SpringerBriefs in Economics

Kobe University Social Science Research Series

The Kobe University Social Science Research Series has been established as a subseries of the SpringerBrief in Economics Series, but in fact this exciting interdisciplinary collection encompasses scholarly research not only in the economics but also in law, political science, business and management, accounting, international relations, and other subdisciplines within the social sciences. As a national university with a special strength in the social sciences, Kobe University actively promotes interdisciplinary research. This series is not limited only to research emerging from Kobe University's faculties of social sciences but also welcomes cross-disciplinary research that integrates studies in the arts and sciences.

Kobe University, founded in 1902, is the second oldest national higher education institution for commerce in Japan and is now a preeminent institution for social science research and education in the country. Currently, the social sciences section includes four faculties—Law, Economics, Business Administration, and International Cooperation Studies—and the Research Institute for Economics and Business Administration (RIEB). There are some 230-plus researchers who belong to these faculties and conduct joint research through the Center for Social Systems Innovation and the Organization for Advanced and Integrated Research, Kobe University.

This book series comprises academic works by researchers in the social sciences at Kobe University as well as their collaborators at affiliated institutions, Kobe University alumni and their colleagues, and renowned scholars from around the world who have worked with academic staff at Kobe University. Although traditionally the research of Japanese scholars has been publicized mainly in the Japanese language, Kobe University strives to promote publication and dissemination of works in English in order to further contribute to the global academic community.

More information about this series at http://www.springer.com/series/15423

Dai Tamada · Philippe Achilleas
Editors

Theory and Practice of Export Control

Balancing International Security and International Economic Relations

Springer

Editors
Dai Tamada
Graduate School of Law
Kobe University
Kobe
Japan

Philippe Achilleas
Institute of Space and Telecommunications Law (IDEST)
University Paris-Sud
Paris
France

ISSN 2191-5504 ISSN 2191-5512 (electronic)
SpringerBriefs in Economics
ISSN 2520-1697 ISSN 2520-1700 (electronic)
Kobe University Social Science Research Series
ISBN 978-981-10-5959-9 ISBN 978-981-10-5960-5 (eBook)
DOI 10.1007/978-981-10-5960-5

Library of Congress Control Number: 2017947477

Printed on acid-free paper

This Springer imprint is published by Springer Nature
The registered company is Springer Nature Singapore Pte Ltd.
The registered company address is: 152 Beach Road, #21-01/04 Gateway East, Singapore 189721, Singapore

The original version of the book was revised: Author affiliation has been updated. The erratum to the book is available at https://doi.org/10.1007/978-981-10-5960-5_14

Contents

Part I
International Regime of Export Control

Chapter 1
Introduction Export Control

Philippe Achilleas

Abstract In a globalized world, the free movement of goods and technologies can lead to the proliferation of weapons and items that can be used for hostile purposes. Thus, free trade may conflict with national or international security. For this reason, it is important to ensure that market opening, supported by international trade law, is not at the expense of the state and people's right to live in a secure environment. To this end, States suppliers of sensitive goods and technologies have adopted export control regimes. An export control regime can be defined as a framework designed to regulate the international trade and transfer of sensitive and critical goods/items and related technologies. The export control regimes have given a new branch of international law which establishes a bridge between international trade law and the law of international security. To master this new regulated trade environment, it is necessary to understand the legal and political basis of the export control regimes as well as the terms of implementation of these schemes.

Keywords Export control · International sanctions · Weapons of mass destruction Conventional weapons · Dual use goods and technology · International trade

In a globalized world, the free movement of goods and technologies can lead to the proliferation of weapons and items that can be used for hostile purposes. Thus, free trade may conflict with national or international security. For this reason, it is important to ensure that the opening of the market, supported by international trade law, does not come at the expense of the State and an individual's right to live in a secure environment. To this end, States supplying sensitive goods and technologies have adopted export control regimes.

An export control regime can be defined as a framework designed to regulate the international trade and transfer of sensitive and critical goods/items and related

P. Achilleas (✉)
Public Law, University Paris Sud, Sceaux, France
e-mail: philippe.achilleas@idest-paris.org; philippe.achilleas@u-psud.fr

P. Achilleas
Institute of Space and Telecommunications Law (IDEST), Sceaux, France

D. Tamada and P. Achilleas (eds.), *Theory and Practice of Export Control*,
Kobe University Social Science Research Series,
DOI 10.1007/978-981-10-5960-5_1

technologies. The objective is to facilitate trade and transfer among friendly and reliable States and prevent hostile and dangerous States, terrorist organizations and individuals from acquiring sensitive items. These regimes can also be implicitly applied by States to protect their economies or to slow the technological development of their enemies or competitors.

These regimes have a very broad scope. Firstly, the concept of export encompasses several kinds of operations: (1) the actual shipment of any goods/items; (2) the transborder electronic or digital transmission of any technology; (3) the release or disclosure, including verbal disclosure, of technology, software or technical data to any foreign national; and (4) the actual use or application of covered technology on behalf of or for the benefit of any foreign entity or person anywhere. Secondly, these programs cover a wide range of items related to weapons of mass destruction, to conventional weapons and dual-use items.

Under these conditions, the persons concerned by these regimes are varied and numerous. On the one hand, these persons are the governments of supplier States of goods and technologies but also the governments of the States affected by the restrictions. On the other hand, exporters are also affected. Exporters include the person who has authority to determine and control the transfer of items out of the country. Of course exporters are first industries, but also public administrations such as technical agencies. Universities may also be considered as exporting entities.

Today the purpose of export control regimes is to prevent security breaches in all its forms. In particular, these regimes aim at preventing the risk of terrorism. However their application extends beyond this objective to include, e.g., the protection of human rights.

The need for security by States has become so important that export control regimes are a key element of international trade in technology goods and services. In addition, these regimes have an impact on the exchange of scientific knowledge including at university level.

As such, export control regimes have led to a new branch of international law which establishes a bridge between international trade law and the law of international security. This new discipline also raises the need to train specialists capable of both understanding the nature and purpose of controlled items and the threats associated with these items. To master this new regulated trade, it is necessary to understand both the legal and political basis of the export control regimes (Sect. 1.1) as well as the terms of implementation of these mechanisms (Sect. 1.2).

1.1 Part I. Establishing Export Regulation Regimes

Export control is organized on the basis of specific regimes adopted by States suppliers of goods and sensitive technologies (Sect. 1.1.1). These regimes are associated with international treaties on disarmament and non-proliferation. In addition to these specific arrangements, export control measures may be based on other mechanisms emanating from general and trade international law (Sect. 1.1.1).

1.1.1 Special Export Control Regimes

International law seeks to govern the international movement of goods and technologies of a military or sensitive nature, and in certain cases, the related know-how through the adoption of special laws and regulations. Originally, the international community sought to combat the proliferation of weapons of mass destruction and their constituents and other closely related matters as these have for many years presented the main threat to international peace and security. It soon became necessary to strengthen controls over conventional weapons and dual-use goods and technologies. This is due to the scale of the traffic of such items between countries over recent years and the destabilizing effect that this trade has on international, regional and national security. This is also due to the possible use of such goods by terrorist groups. The establishment of export control regimes addresses the need to strengthen the non proliferation of such military and sensitive goods and technologies. Export control regimes are related both to weapons of mass destruction (1) and conventional arms and dual-use (2).

1. **Regimes related to weapons of mass destruction**

Weapons of mass destruction are designed to kill civilians as well as military personnel on a large scale. Although no universally accepted legal definition exists, weapons of mass destruction are often classified under the acronym "NBC": nuclear, biological and chemical weapons. In the area of weapons of mass destruction, export control mechanisms rely on conventional regimes.

It is useful to distinguish regimes dealing with nuclear activities from regimes dealing with biological and chemical activities.

Nuclear weapons are derived from atomic energy. During the Second World War, the USA launched two atomic bombs. The first bomb hit Hiroshima on 6 August 1945 and the second hit Nagasaki on 9 August 1945. After the war, the proliferation of the atomic bomb allowed other countries to acquire similar technology: Russia (1949), Great Britain (1952), France (1960), China (1964), India (1974), Israel (almost certainly since 1979) and Pakistan (1998). Since the 1950s, the international community has decided to limit nuclear weapons by banning nuclear testing[1] and proliferation of such weapons. The legal foundation for the non-proliferation policy is the Treaty on the Non-Proliferation of Nuclear Weapons (NPT) which opened for signature on 1 July 1968.[2] From this point of view, the NPT represents a bargain between the Non-Nuclear-Weapon States (NNWS) and the Nuclear-Weapon States (NWS).[3] Indeed, based on Article II, the NWS agree

[1]The banning of nuclear testing is based on international conventions: the Treaty Banning Nuclear Weapon Tests in the Atmosphere, in Outer Space and Under Water signed on 5 August 1963 (480 *UNTS* 43) and the Comprehensive Nuclear-Test-Ban Treaty, signed on 24 September 1996 (UN document A/50/1027).

[2]729 *UNTS* 161.

[3]NWS are the following: China, France, Russia, the United Kingdom and the United States.

not to transfer nuclear weapons technology or other nuclear explosive devices to NNWS and NNWS accept not to manufacture or acquire nuclear weapons and not to seek or receive any assistance in this field. In return, Article IV of the NPT states that all Parties have the inalienable right to develop the research, production and use of nuclear energy for peaceful purposes without discrimination. To this end, Articles IV and V of the Treaty encourage the international transfer of nuclear goods and technologies for civilian uses on a non-discriminatory basis.

The sovereign right to civilian nuclear motivates the establishment of export control regimes. It is thus vital for the international community to ensure that nuclear items and technology transferred for peaceful purposes are not diverted for military purposes. A first regime was established in 1971 following the coming into force of the NPT: the Zangger[4] Committee. It is composed of suppliers or potential suppliers of nuclear material and equipment. The main objective of the regime is to interpret and implement NPT Article III, par. 2 according to which NWS undertake not to provide source or special fissionable material, or equipment or material especially designed or prepared for the processing, use or production of special fissionable material, to any NNWS for peaceful purposes, unless the source or special fissionable material shall be subject to the safeguards set forth in an agreement negotiated and concluded with the International Atomic Energy Agency (IAEA). The regime focuses only on source material and special fissionable material. Following the explosion in 1974 of a nuclear device by India, States decided to establish a second regime called Nuclear Suppliers Group (NSG) to ensure that nuclear trade for peaceful purposes will not contribute to the proliferation of nuclear explosive devices. The Indian test has indeed demonstrated that certain non-weapons specific nuclear technology could be readily turned to weapons development. For this reason, the NSG focuses on the transfer of any item and technology that are especially designed or prepared for nuclear use but also on the transfer of nuclear related dual-use items and technologies.

The regimes on control of international transfers related to chemicals and biological weapons are also based on a non-proliferation convention: the Convention on the prohibition of the development, production and stockpiling of bacteriological (biological) and toxin weapons and on their destruction[5] signed on 10 April 1972 and the Convention on the prohibition of the development, production, stockpiling and use of chemical weapons and on their destruction[6] signed on 13 January 1993. These two conventions prohibit States to develop, produce, acquire, stockpile, retain chemical weapons or transfer chemical as well as microbial or other biological agents or toxins weapons. They also prohibit the use of such items for military purposes.[7] These conventions also state that each party has the right to

---

[4]Prof. Claude Zangger was the first Chairman of the Committee.

[5]1015 *UNTS* 163.

[6]1974 *UNTS* 45.

[7]Article I of the Convention of the biological Convention; Article I of the Convention on chemical weapons.

develop, produce, otherwise acquire, retain, transfer and use chemicals as well as microbial or other biological agents or toxins for peaceful uses. As a consequence, States have to control that international transfers of such goods and technologies are carried on for purposes not prohibited.[8] After the UN concluded in 1984 that Iraq had used chemical weapons during the Iran-Iraq War, Australia proposed the organization of a conference of States to adopt a framework for controlling the export of chemical products. Since 1985, this informal group of States, known as the Australia Group, has been meeting every year to enhance cooperation in the field of chemical and biological weapons prohibition. The regime deals respectively with: chemical weapons precursors, dual-use chemical manufacturing and equipment and related technology; dual-use biological equipment; biological agents, plants pathogens and animal pathogens.

The international regimes on the non-proliferation of weapons of mass destruction are only effective to the extent they also deal with the transfer of weapons delivery systems. These systems are either aircraft (with or without pilots), or missiles, in particular ballistic and cruise missiles. There is no international treaty dealing with the non-proliferation of missiles and other delivery systems. The Hague Code of Conduct against Ballistic Missile Proliferation[9]—adopted on 25 November 2002—represents the first attempt to establish measures for all States to prevent and curb the proliferation of ballistic missile systems capable of delivering weapons of mass destruction. This gentlemen's agreement sets out the broad lines of policy cooperation in this field, including the principle of non-proliferation. Despite the absence of an international non-proliferation treaty, States have adopted an export control regime. Thus, in 1987, governments decided to set up the Missile Technology Control Regime (MTCR). This informal agreement controls international transfers that could make a contribution to delivery systems other than manned aircraft. The regime is focused on complete rocket and unmanned aerial vehicle systems (including ballistic missiles, space launch vehicles, sounding rockets, cruise missiles, target drones, and reconnaissance drones), their major complete subsystems (such as rocket stages, engines, guidance sets, and re-entry vehicles), and related software and technology.

2. **Regime on conventional weapons and dual-use items**

Each State has the right to produce, sell or buy any weapons which are not prohibited by law, so called conventional weapons. This right fits with two fundamental principles of international law recognized by the Charter of the United Nations adopted on 26 June 1945[10]: a country's right of legitimate self-defence[11]

[8]Article III of the Convention on biological weapons; Article VI of the Convention on chemical weapons.

[9]Not published.

[10]1 *UNTS* XVI.

[11]Article 51 of the UN Charter.

and the right of sovereignty on economic and security matters.[12] The proliferation of conventional weapons does however still represent a threat to international peace and security for several reasons: (1) a potential destabilization of areas where tension and regional conflict threaten international and national security; (2) an effect on the progress of the peaceful social and economic development of all peoples; and (3) a danger of increasing illicit and covert arms trafficking.

The international community therefore committed itself to cooperate on the issues of the non-proliferation of conventional weapons and dual-use technologies. In 1950, some States decided to establish the Coordinating Committee for Multilateral Export Controls (COCOM), an informal organization in order to restrict the export of sensitive items that could be used to contribute to military potential and the proliferation of weapons systems. During the Cold War, the COCOM was, in fact, designed to impose an embargo on Western States' exports on Socialist Countries. At the end of the Cold War, members of the COCOM recognized that East-West focus was no longer the appropriate basis for export controls and decided to adopt a new framework. COCOM ceased to exist in March 1994 and the Wassenaar Arrangement was adopted in order to contribute to international security and stability, by promoting transparency and greater responsibility in transfers of conventional arms and dual-use goods and technologies.

1.1.2 General Regimes as Basis for Export Regulation

Besides the export control mechanisms, there are other rules of international law which can establish export restrictions. These restrictions are based on the one hand on the regime of international sanctions (1) and, on the other, on security exceptions allowed by the international trade law (2).

1. **International sanctions**

Sanctions are tools used by countries or international organizations to persuade a particular entity or group of entities to change their policy or at least to demonstrate a country's opinion about the other's policies. The objectives of sanctions can be divided into several categories: conflict resolution; non-proliferation; counter-terrorism; promotion of democarty; and protection of civilians (including human rights).

International sanctions may be divided in several categories. Firstly, diplomatic sanctions include practices such as recalling of embassy and consular staff, non-recognition of a particular government and suspension of cultural relations. Secondly, military sanctions cover the use of force against a country and arms embargoes to cut off supplies of arms or dual-use items. Thirdly, economic sanctions seek to restrict trade and other economic activity with a country. Economic

[12]Article 2 of the UN Charter.

sanctions may apply to dealings with entire countries, non-state actors, such as terrorist organizations, or designated persons from a target country. Economic sanctions can take many forms: import/export restrictions; financial prohibition; asset freeze; travel ban; or asset freeze.

International sanctions should not be mistaken for export control regimes to the extent that the purpose of sanctions is to restrict international trade while the objective of the export control regimes is to regulate exports.

International sanctions can have as a legal basis Article 41 of the Chapter VII of the UN Charter which covers enforcement measures not involving the use of armed force. Article 41 States: "The Security Council may decide what measures not involving the use of armed force are to be employed to give effect to its decisions, and it may call upon the Members of the United Nations to apply such measures. These may include complete or partial interruption of economic relations and of rail, sea, air, postal, telegraphic, radio, and other means of communication, and the severance of diplomatic relations". The Security Council first imposed mandatory sanctions in relation with the unrecognized State of Rhodesia [resolution 253 (1968)] and apartheid of South Africa [resolution 418 (1977)]. UN members are obliged to follow the decisions of the Security Council imposing sanctions.

The Iranian example represents a case study for UN sanctions. Between 2006 and 2010, the UN Security Council imposed four rounds of sanctions against Iran in response to the proliferation risks presented by Iran's nuclear program in light of Iran's failure to meet the requirements of the IAEA and to comply with the provisions of earlier Security Council resolutions. Acting under Chapter VII of the Charter, the Security Council adopted resolutions 1737 (2006), 1747 (2007), 1803 (2008) and 1929 (2010). These sanctions resulted in a broad prohibition on exports and imports to and from Iran, subject to certain exceptions, and on financial transactions. Diplomatic efforts to reach a comprehensive solution to the Iranian nuclear issue culminated in the Joint Comprehensive Plan of Action (JCPOA) concluded on 14 July 2015 by China, France, Germany, the Russian Federation, the United Kingdom, the United States, the European Union and Iran. On 20 July 2015, the Security Council adopted resolution 2231 (2015) endorsing the JCPOA. The text promotes the development of normal economic and trade relations and cooperation with Iran and resulted in significant sanctions relief for Iran.

However, sanctions may be taken in the absence of a UN decision. This situation occurs particularly when one of the permanent members of the Security Council is opposed to the adoption of a resolution establishing sanctions. Sanctions are then taken on a decentralized basis. In this case, States and international organizations, such as the EU, determine for themselves in the first instance if a country/organization has violated international law, and proceed to impose sanctions against it. For example, in 2014, in response to the annexation of Crimea by the Russian Federation, some governments and international organizations, led by the United States and European Union, imposed sanctions on Russian individuals and trade. In response, Russia adopted reciprocal sanctions especially against the United States, the EU, Norway, Canada and Australia. Such unilateral actions, called "countermeasures" are not prohibited under international law but are strictly controlled. They fall under the law of the international responsibility of States and international organizations. Thus, an injured State or international organization may take countermeasures only against a State or an international organization which is responsible for an internationally wrongful act in order to induce that State/international organization to comply with its obligations to repair the injury caused.[13] International law also authorizes countermeasures by non-injured States/international organizations in two situations: (1) if the obligation breached is owed to a group of States or international organizations, including the State or organization that invokes responsibility, and is established for the protection of a collective interest of the group; (2) if the obligation breached is owed to the international community as a whole.[14]

2. WTO security exception

Any restrictions on international trade in goods and services may represent a violation of the World Trade Organization (WTO) agreements signed in Marrakesh on 15 April 1994. Indeed, such practices are contrary to the basic principles of the General Agreement on Tariffs and Trade (GATT),[15] which regulates trade in goods and the General Agreements on Trade in Services (GATS),[16] which regulates the trade in services. First, WTO members implementing export control regimes may violate of the so-called "most favored nation principle" provided for in Articles I of the GATT and 2 of the GATS. This rule imposes an absence of discrimination between WTO members. Second, export control is akin to a non-tariff barrier to trade in goods contrary to GATT. From this viewpoint, export control measures would be contrary to GATT Article VIII on fees and formalities connected with importation and exportation of which paragraph 1 (c) establishes a general duty to minimize the incidence and complexity of import and export formalities. Export control would also be contrary to GATT Article X imposing application of domestic trade regulations, including those impacting importation and exportation, in a uniform, impartial and reasonable manner.

However, WTO law recognizes the possibility of restricting trade relations for security reasons.

Article XXI b of the GATT and Article XIV bis b of the GATS provide: "Nothing in this Agreement shall be construed [...] to prevent any contracting party from taking any action which it considers necessary for the protection of its

[13]Article 49 of the 2001 Articles on Responsibility of States for Internationally Wrongful Acts (Annex to General Assembly resolution 56/83 of 12 December 2001 as corrected by the document A/56/49(Vol. I)/Corr. 4) and 51 of the 2011 Draft articles on the responsibility of international organizations (*Yearbook of the International Law Commission, 2011*, vol. II, Part Two).

[14]See Articles 54 and 48 of the 2001 Articles on Responsibility of States for Internationally Wrongful Acts and Articles 57 and 49 of the 2011 Draft articles on the responsibility of international organizations of the of the 2011 Draft articles on the responsibility of international organizations.

[15]1867 *UNTS* 187.

[16]1869 *UNTS* 183.

essential security interests (i) relating to fissionable materials or the materials from which they are derived; (ii) relating to the traffic in arms, ammunition and implements of war and to such traffic in other goods and materials as is carried on directly or indirectly for the purpose of supplying a military establishment; (iii) taken in time of war or other emergency in international relations [...]". It is accepted that, both in their formulation as their purpose, these articles allow each member a broad margin of appreciation in deciding whether a situation falls within the protection of its essential security interests and in identifying the action necessary to take.[17] That is why the USA justifies their export control policies on the basis of this article.[18]

1.2 Implementing Export Control Regimes

The implementation of export control regimes are based on both technical and political considerations. It takes the form of a set of texts which aim to identify sensitive technologies and countries that pose a threat. This implementation is exercised at two levels since the regimes are defined internationally, but applied nationally (Sect. 1.2.1). Thus, governments and States are directly involved. Indeed, these entities are responsible for the control. The effectiveness of control involves the implementation of complex, expensive and risky procedures (Sect. 1.2.2).

1.2.1 A Method in Two Steps

Each export control regime is implemented by a method combining an international approach and a national approach. Initially, the partners get together to define and modify elements of the regime (1). Then, they apply the system on the basis of national law and European law for Member States of the European Union (2).

1. **International cooperation**

International cooperation is established by the adoption of concerted non-conventional acts. These documents are signed by several subjects of international law such as treaties. However, they have no binding force. They represent the basis of a political commitment of the signatories. Each regime is based on several documents. First, members adopt lists of items to be controlled. Then, they adopt guidelines to clarify the criteria for exercising the control.

Thus, export control regimes are organized around the following international texts.

---

[17]OMC 1995.

[18]See for example: Executive Order 13222 2001.

- Zangger Committee
  - Guidelines for implementing the export control provisions of the Nuclear Nonproliferation Treaty [Article III(2)] (1974).[19]
  - List on the designation of items of equipment or material especially designed or prepared for the processing, use or production of special fissionable material,[20] known as the "Trigger List" (1974).[21]
- Nuclear Suppliers Group
  - Guidelines for Nuclear Transfers and list of controlled items (1974, rev. 2013).[22]
  - Guidelines for Transfers of Nuclear-Related Dual-Use Equipment, Materials, Software and Related Technology and list of controlled items (1992, rev. 2013).[23]
- Australia Group
  - Guidelines For Transfers of Sensitive Chemical or Biological Items (2002, rev. 2015)[24]
  - Common Control Lists: Chemical Weapons Precursors; Dual-use chemical manufacturing facilities and equipment and related technology and software; Dual-use biological equipment and related technology and software; Human and Animal Pathogens and Toxins; and Plant pathogens[25] (rev. 2015).
- MTCR
  - Guidelines for Sensitive Missile-Relevant Transfers (1987, rev. 2013)[26]
  - The Equipment, Software and Technology Annex (1987, rev. 2013)[27]
- Wassenaar Arrangement
  - Guidelines and Procedures, including the Initial Elements (1996, rev. 2015)[28]
  - Lists of Dual-Use Goods and Technologies (1996, rev. 2016)[29]
  - Munitions List (1996, rev. 2016)[30]

---

[19] IAEA, INFCIRC/209, Appendix, 3 September 1974, Memorandum A.

[20] IAEA, INFCIRC/209, Appendix, 3 September 1974, Memorandum B.

[21] The list of controlled items developed by the Zangger Committee is known as the "Trigger List" because export of those items triggers IAEA safeguards.

[22] IAEA, INFCIRC/254/Rev.12/Part 1, 13 November 2013 (last version).

[23] IAEA, INFCIRC/254/Rev.9/Part 2, 13 November 2013 (last version).

[24] Available on the website of the Australia Group: www.australiagroup.net/en/guidelines.html.

[25] Available on the website of the Australia Group: www.australiagroup.net/en/controllists.html.

[26] 26 *ILM* 599 (1987).

[27] MTCR/TEM/2015/Annex, 8 October 2015 (last version).

[28] Avalable on the website of the Wassenaar Arrangement: www.wassenaar.org/public-documents.

[29] WA-LIST (15) 1 Corr.1* 04-04-2016.

[30] Idem.

The lists represent the core element of each regime. In-depth knowledge of the lists is essential for the effective implementation of the law on export control. The lists cover both military and dual-use items. These documents are amended regularly to take account of developments in technology. Motivations to exercise control also evolve with new threats. Originally the regimes were aimed at avoiding preventing States acting in a manner detrimental to international peace and security from having access to sensitive items. Today, they also impose controls in order to combat crime, terrorism and human rights violation.

The regimes also establish mechanisms of cooperation among the participants. These mechanisms include: exchange of information; survey of participants application of the guidelines; consultation on specific sensitive cases; and regular meetings and secretariat.

2. **National implementation**

The export control regimes are being implemented within the framework of national law.

Participants thus undertake to introduce into their legal systems the guidelines and lists of items to be controlled. They must first establish or designate an administrative authority to organize control. Participants must also establish two lists: one for military items; the other for dual-use goods and technologies. The administration will have the responsibility to issue licenses authorizing the international transfer. In practice, if an item is classified either in the national lists or attached to a decision imposing sanctions on a State or its citizens, the administration authorizes the transfer after a reasoning in three steps: (1) who is the end user —Country/person?; (2) what is the purpose of the transfer (end use)?; and (3) what are the product characteristics (performance criteria)? The administration also determines what are the main commercial intermediaries and the funding modes of the transfer. If the transfer is a risk to international security and stability, license should be refused. Finally, participants agree to sanction any person who carries out a transfer without having asked the license or in violation of a license refusal.

The export control measures also have an extraterritorial application. Thus, the issued export licenses generally contain re-export provisions. Under these provisions, the end user located in the importing country must obtain permission from the administration that issued the license to re-export the authorized item. Americans go further into the extraterritorial application of their export control regulations. Indeed, they consider that, once an authorized American component is incorporated in equipment, the complete equipment is subject to US law. It is as if the foreign equipment if "contaminated" by the US component. Therefore, the export of the equipment is subject to a dual authorization. The first is issued by the national administration. The second is issued by the US administration. This "contamination" theory is contrary to international law. Indeed, it represents a violation of the sovereignty of the State of the exporting entity.

Thus, US law is a central element in the international export control. The American regulation is based on two regimes. The arms trade falls under the *Export*

Control Act of 1976[31] and the International Traffic in Arms Regulations (ITAR). It is administered by the Department of State (Office of Defense Trade Controls) which applies the United States Munitions List (USML). The list includes 21 categories. Trade in dual-use goods falls under the Export Administration Act of 1979[32] and the Export Administration Regulations (EAR). It is administered by the Department of Commerce (Bureau of Export Administration) that applies the Commerce Control List (CCL). The list includes 10 categories.

The European Union also has an export control regime for its Member States. The arms trade is the subject of a Common Position 2008/944/CFSP of 8 December 2008 defining common rules governing control of exports of military technology and equipment.[33] States are also subject to the Directive 2009/81/EC on defense and sensitive security procurement of 13 July 2009.[34] The trade in dual-use goods is a direct competence of the EU. As a consequence, it is submitted to the Council Regulation (EC) No 428/2009 of 5 May 2009 setting up a Community regime for the control of exports, transfer, brokering and transit of dual-use items.[35] The regime organizes the free movement of dual-use goods and technologies within the EU (except items listed in Annex IV). The text maintains the obligation of national authorization for export outside the EU.

The implementation of the export control regimes at the national level is not only the responsibility of governments. In fact, the control is carried out primarily at the exporter level. With the development of export control regimes, companies have gone from free trade to a controlled trade. The first consequence is the establishment of a service dedicated to export control within each undertaking. This implies that the company has trained staff on this complex discipline. Companies must also implement special internal procedures. Drafting contracts should include export control clauses. These measures are very important since companies risk penalties in case of non-compliance with regulations of export controls. As stated, these measures also apply to public agencies and universities.

In reality, the implementation of export control regimes greatly affects the economic and scientific actors working in sensitive sectors. These regimes do not translate only the prohibition of transferring assets, but also technology and knowledge. So any preliminary negotiations on a program or a project with a foreign country may need an authorization. Similarly, exchanges by mail or telephone shall be controlled. Within an entity, staff may be excluded from some projects because of their nationality. Technological and scientific universities also have constraints to refuse certain courses or internships to students from countries considered at risk.

---

[31] 22 *USC* 2778.

[32] *PL* 96–72.

[33] *OJEU* L 335, 13 December 2008, p. 99.

[34] *OJEU* L 216, 20 August 2009, p. 76.

[35] *OJEU* L 326, 29 May 2009, p. 134.

1.2.2 *Effectiveness*

Two issues call the effectiveness of export control regimes into question. On the one hand they are at risk for States and exporters (1). On the other hand, they have some limitations (2).

1. **Risks**

Firstly, the risks related to the implementation of export control regimes are economic and commercial. Thus, these regimes have an effect on the competitiveness of the industries concerned. This effect is linked to cumbersome, complicated and expensive procedures necessary for the export of sensitive goods and technologies. Another cause is the refusal to license imposed by the administration. Under these conditions, companies can lose business in the international market. Thus, US technology companies have long suffered from a strict application of export controls in the United States. They were absent from some strategic markets, such as China, while European firms were winning many contracts.

Secondly, implementation of export control regimes includes legal risks. Indeed, these regimes may violate some well-established legal principles. Thus, export control may be contrary to the economic freedoms by imposing restrictions on the free movement of goods, capital and persons as well as restrictions on freedom to provide services. Export control can also affect the right of foreign investment since it can hamper economic activity of foreign companies established in the territory. By blocking the transfer of technology and knowledge to some countries, export control regimes may also infringe the right to development of States. Certain rules relating to human rights may also be affected. Thus, by limiting access to information and knowledge of certain people because of their nationality, the implementation of export controls, if disproportionate, is contrary to the freedom of information or the right to education. Another point should be mentioned. By blocking the development of space projects by some States, the implementation of export control rules represent a restriction on the freedom of space, which is a fundamental principle of space law. Lastly, we saw that the extraterritorial application of US law violates the principle of sovereignty.

2. **Limitations**

Firstly the export control regimes present exceptions. For example, they are not applicable to goods and technologies freely available in the market.

Second, the control mechanisms have inherent technical limits. To the extent that the regimes do not list all goods and technologies, it is possible to export/import items that are not on the lists. For example, the European-based company Thales Alenia Space, has developed satellites containing no US component. These satellites so-called "ITAR-free" can be sold to China, while US companies cannot sell satellites to this country. Since the listed items are often associated with performance criteria, it is also possible to bypass control regimes provisions by degrading the performance of listed goods and technologies. This situation requires the regime members to regularly review the lists. They can also use the so called "catch-all" provision. This provision allows the control a non-listed item, in particular, in application of decision of the UN Security Council or the Council of the European Union (for EU members).[36] Finally, it is necessary to take into account new risks linked to the transfer of sensitive data by electronic communication networks, especially the Internet.

Third, export control regimes have policy limits. It is possible to slow technological development, but not to prevent a state to drive its policy. For example, despite a strict control imposed by the USA on international transfers to China, China continues its technical development. The regimes also failed to prevent the development of a nuclear program in Iran or North Korea. This reality is more serious for international security. As we have seen, it is the sanctions imposed by the UN have stopped the Iranian military nuclear program.

Thus, risks and limitations presented here allow to question the effectiveness of the export control regimes. Certainly the effectiveness of such regimes depends on their proportionate application to a legitimate aim. Otherwise, administrations and exporters risks to be paralyzed by the multiplication of procedures. Under these conditions, the search for international security would generate commercial insecurity detrimental to the development of exporting and importing States.

References

Executive Order 13222. 2001. Continuation of Export Control Regulations. *Federal Register* 66 (163).

OMC. 1995. *GATT Analytical Index—Guide to GATT Law and Practice*, volume 1, Geneva, 1995, pp. 599–10.

[36]*Wasseanaar Arrangement, Statement of Understanding on Control of Non-Listed Dual-Use Items*, adopted during the Plenary Meeting in 2003; Article 4 of the EU Regulation 428/2009.

Chapter 2
Embargoes and International Sanctions from an Industry Perspective

Romain Broner

Embargoes and other coercive measures have been in existence since Antiquity. One of the first documented international embargoes dates back to the IXth century in Western Europe, when the Emperor Charlemagne (Charles the Great) decided to forbid the selling and exportation of Frank swords outside the Frank Empire, as well as preventing Frank blacksmiths from travelling abroad. These swords were made of an alloy of steel that made them light, flexible and solid. The decision was confirmed by Charlemagne's grandson Charles the Bald in the Edict of Pistres in 864. This is one of the first export control legal acts.

2.1 Coercive Measures: Tools for International Relations

Countries violating their international obligations, in particular when committing unlawful acts are responsible and expose themselves to the imposition of coercive measures that may include, among other things, embargoes and other international sanctions. Coercive measures may also encompass the sending of military troops (for peacekeeping missions, military intervention, blockade, etc.), the temporary or definitive suspension of diplomatic relations, or customs and trade barriers. The imposition of international sanctions is one of the most useful and adaptive tools in international relations.

This communication reflects solely the views of its author and does not express the views of his employer or the University Paris-Sud.

R. Broner (✉)
Airbus Helicopters, 1, Place Armand Carrel, 75019 Paris, France
e-mail: romain.broner@gmail.com

D. Tamada and P. Achilleas (eds.), *Theory and Practice of Export Control*,
Kobe University Social Science Research Series,
DOI 10.1007/978-981-10-5960-5_2

By imposing sanctions, a country or an international organization, such as the United Nations—although some other international bodies may decide the imposition of sanctions—has several objectives:

- Put pressure on the opposite party (or country) in the framework of bilateral or multilateral negotiations;
- Urge the opposite party to cease an infringement of international law;
- Impose international pressure with regard to the country's internal situation, especially in case of important human rights or humanitarian law violations.

Coercive measures may be comprehensive but most are targeted and designed as a middle step between international protestations and armed intervention. They are also seen as a credible alternative, especially for countries that have limited military capacities but important economic ties with the country under consideration. Coercive measures must consequently be considered as a political tool that is mainly used for diplomatic purposes.

All countries are entitled to impose international sanctions, but most embargoes are decided by the United Nations Security Council (UNSC) or regional organisations such as the European Union (EU). They are then enforced collectively by Member States to enhance their efficiency. However, some international sanctions are unilateral, such as the trade restrictions imposed by the United States of America against Cuba.[1]

Correct and effective implementation of international sanctions call for a holistic approach that must involve all relevant stakeholders, and more particularly both public and private sectors, as well as Non-Governmental Organisations, the media, multinational companies, and public opinion. Such an approach is particularly requested in order to ensure a coordinated and efficient implementation and enforcement of sanctions, avoid collateral and undesired effects (both humanitarian and economic), and assess the impact on international law and diplomacy.

2.2 Coercive Measures and Effectiveness: Balancing the Consequences

Coercive measures are designed to force the opposite party to abide by its international obligations. However, the imposition of international sanctions requires elaborating and implementing a strategy based on the effects to be realized.

- Conflict resolution, including intra-state conflicts (e.g. Democratic Republic of the Congo, Cote d'Ivoire). The aim of such sanctions is to weaken one or both of the parties to the conflict in order to allow military defeat, to create an

[1]See in particular the Cuban Democracy Act of 1992 (22 U.S.C. chapter 69) and the Helms-Burton Act of 1996 (22 U.S.C. chapter 69a).

incentive for negotiation or cease-fire, or to enforce the implementation of a peace agreement.
- Protection of civilians (e.g. Somalia, Sudan). The imposition of sanctions may also prevent or stop massive human rights violations or at least limit as much as possible the opposing party's funding and supplying of weapons and ammunitions.
- Counter-terrorism (e.g. sanctions against Al-Qaeda, Hezbollah). Quite similarly, the purpose of sanctions can be to limit terrorist organizations' capabilities and financing, as well as promote justice and accountability.
- Democratisation (e.g. Iraq, Guinea-Bissau). In countries subject to military dictatorship or after a coup, embargoes and sanctions may be necessary to put international pressure on the country under consideration and ease democratic transition, and if necessary create some incentive for the restoration of constitutional order.
- Non-proliferation (e.g. North Korea, Iran). Probably one of the most sensitive categories of embargoes, although difficult to enforce efficiently. Such sanctions are designed to constrain the ability of a country to develop—or help develop—nuclear, chemical and biological weapons, as well as ballistic missiles. These sanctions regimes are mostly based on Non Proliferation Treaty (NPT)[2] enforcement.

Once the strategy—or the goals—has been established, international sanctions can rely on a set of different coercive measures that allow maximizing the effects while balancing with potential drawbacks. To this end, arms embargoes (including export, import, transfer, brokering, associated services, financing, etc.) are one of the most effective tools with a very limited negative impact on the country's population or economic resources. Such embargoes are strong political signals and are widely used, especially by the United Nations or the European Union, in most of the sanctions regimes currently in place.

Travel ban and assets freeze (including financial sanctions) are also relatively common and easy to implement. However, the imposition of financial sanctions against a country needs a particularly wide international cooperation in order to enhance its efficiency. Such sanctions may also have an adverse impact on the country's population and economy and include the severance of diplomatic relations.

Finally, trade restrictions that can extend from rare resources to strategic goods such as nuclear devices, food, or oil and gas are the most comprehensive coercive measures and can be assimilated to boycott. Such sanctions may have an important impact on the country's population and need to be carefully balanced and targeted in order to limit their negative side effects.

---

[2]The Treaty on the Non-Proliferation of Nuclear Weapons is an international treaty aiming at preventing the proliferation of nuclear weapons and related weapons technology and to promote cooperation in the peaceful use of nuclear energy. The treaty was signed on 1 July 1968 in New York (United States) and entered into force on 5 March 1970.

Every sanctions regime is unique, with a specific purpose, timing, and consequences that may vary in time in order to ensure an effective and useful application. Proper sequencing of the different types of sanctions, as well as the implementation and enforcement mechanisms are essential to establish efficient embargoes with positive political and diplomatic outcomes.

2.3 Legal Framework of International Sanctions

Coercive measures and embargoes date back to the Antiquity. However, during the XXth and XXIst centuries, and more particularly since the end of the Cold War era, international sanctions have been widely used in different situations. Sanctions can be decided by international organisations such as the United Nations Security Council (UNSC), the European Union, the Economic Community of Western African States (ECOWAS), and the Organization for the Security and Cooperation in Europe (OSCE), or by individual states that may decide to enforce unilateral embargoes worldwide, such as the United States of America.

After the First World War, the League of Nations[3] was tasked with maintaining international peace and enforcing international obligations by common actions,[4] as well as taking ‘any action that may be deemed wise and effectual to safeguard the peace of nations’.[5] Although this allowed the League of Nations under Article 16 of the Covenant to impose the ‘severance of all trade and financial relations’, as well as the ‘prevention of all financial commercial or personal intercourse between the nationals of the Covenant-breaking State and the nationals of any other State’, such financial, economic and diplomatic measures were inconsistently applied until the third decade of the twentieth century.

The United Nations legal framework. Since the Second World War and the creation of the United Nations,[6] coercive measures may be decided by the United Nations Security Council (UNSC) as a political body. They are mainly imposed under the United Nations’ Charter Chapter VII that allows the Security Council to take actions and not only formulate recommendations. Such actions may include

[3]The League of Nations was an intergovernmental organization founded in 1920, following the Paris Peace Conference that ended the First World War. Its principal mission was to maintain world peace through collective security and disarmament and settling international disputes through negotiation and arbitration.

[4]Article 8 of the Covenant of the League of Nations, signed on 28 June 1919 in Paris (France) and effective on 10 January 1920.

[5]*Ibid.*, art. 11.

[6]The United Nations is an intergovernmental organization established in 1945 as a replacement for the ineffective League of Nations to promote and preserve international peace and cooperation. The United Nations Charter was signed on 26 June 1946 in San Francisco (United States) and entered into force on 24 October 1946.

the use of armed force, but also encompass binding economic sanctions or arms embargoes.

Under Article 39 of the UN Charter, the UNSC may interfere when a certain international situation represents a 'threatening against peace, an encroachment of peace, or an aggression act'. In such cases, the UNSC is entitled to impose political and economic measures, either without (art. 41) or with (art. 42) the use of military force. According to the Charter, such actions 'may include'—but are not limited to—blockade, complete or partial interruption of economic relations, severance of diplomatic relations, etc.

The UN Charter does not specify under which situations sanctions must be applied, or the types of measures to be implemented, leaving room for interpretation and adaptation by the UNSC to implement effective measures tailored to the situation under consideration rather than imposing mandatory coercive actions such as an arms embargo. Most sanctions regimes are decided under Article 41, without the use of armed force.

Since international sanctions imposed by the UNSC under Chapter VII are compulsory for United Nations Member States, effectiveness can only be reached through international cooperation and global implementation. One of the first mandatory broad sanctions to be imposed by the UNSC consisted of Resolutions 181 & 182 (1963) and 418 (1977) against the South African Apartheid regime. The sanctions (military embargo) were decided in response to the political system of Apartheid, its regional military aggression in the Southern African sub-region, and the pursuit of a nuclear weapons program by the Government of South Africa. Several sanctions regimes were later implemented, mainly focusing or restricting weapons trade and nuclear-related sanctions (cf. UNSC Resolution 661 (1990) against Iraq).

In the 1990s, the UNSC started to establish more targeted sanctions in order to reduce as much as possible the negative consequences of comprehensive sanctions regimes [cf. Liberia—Res. 788 (1992), Rwanda—Res. 918 (1994), or Yugoslavia/Kosovo—Res. 1160 (1999)]. Targeted sanctions were designed to minimize humanitarian impact that might result from comprehensive sanctions, as well as improve efficiency and targeting of sanctions that proved to be ineffective when too broad.

Finally, and more specifically since 2000, sanctions are designed to target States (including failed States) as well as non-state actors, extending from rebel groups and arms dealers to terrorist organizations and decision-making individuals that threaten peace. Although fine-tuning international sanctions in order to better target the effects to be obtained and to minimize unintended side effects is certainly an improvement, such sanctions proved to be far more difficult to implement in an effective way, especially regarding their financial aspects and consequences for other countries.

2.4 The European Union Legal Framework

From the European Union perspective, international sanctions are called restrictive measures. The European Union enforces embargoes and sanctions decided by the UNSC (of which two European Union member States, France and the United Kingdom, are permanent members,). However, the European Union may also impose autonomous measures as part of its Common Foreign and Security Policy (CFSP). Restrictive measures, from the European Union's perspective, are part of a global toolkit necessary to bring a change in policy or activity by the opposite party that can be a foreign country or Government, or dedicated entities or individual.

Legal basis. The legal basis for the European Union to impose restrictive measures—and have them enforced by its 28 Member States—lies in both the Treaty of the European Union (TUE) and the Treaty on the Functioning of the European Union (TFUE).

- Under Article 21§2 of the TUE, the advancement of 'democracy, rule of law, human rights and the principles of international law', as well as the preservation of peace and international security, the respect of the United Nations Charter and the international law are under the competence of the European Union Council,[7] as part of the European Union's external actions. The external action of the European Union is coordinated by the High Representative of the Union for Foreign Affairs and Security Policy, currently Ms. Federica Mogherini from Italy.
- Under articles 30 and 31 of the TUE,[8] all matters linked to the European Union's Common Foreign and Security Policy (CFSP) may be referred to the European Union Council. Such matters include the imposition of restrictive measures as part of the Union's foreign policy.
- Under Article 215 of the Treaty on the Functioning of the European Union,[9] the imposition of restrictive measures is decided by the EU Council, with proper information of the EU Parliament and the EU Commission, especially when the said measures necessitate the adoption of a legal act by the EU Council—i.e. the 'interruption or reduction, in part of completely, of economic and financial relations with one or more third countries'.
- Finally, under Article 275, the Court of Justice of the European Union has jurisdiction to review the legality of decisions providing restrictive measures against natural or legal persons adopted by the EU Council. Under Article 275, several blacklisted natural or legal entities were removed from the listing for lack of legal grounds.

---

[7]Treaty of the European Union, Official Journal of the European Union C 326/13 of 26 October 2012, art. 21 (p. 16).

[8]*Ibid.* (p. 18).

[9]Treaty on the Functioning of the European Union, Official Journal of the European Union No. C326/47 of 26 October 2012, art. 215 (p. 98).

Consequently, restrictive measures as foreign relations decisions are under the responsibility of the EU Council, along with implementing regulation necessary for economic and financial sanctions, while travel bans and arms embargoes do not need additional implementation measures to be applied by EU Member States. The EU Council and the High Representative are key players, with important inputs from the EU Parliament and Commission, especially for economic and financial aspects (EU Commission), as well as for Human Rights and other political aspects (EU Parliament), whereas the EU Court of Justice is entitled to ensure compliance of acts resulting from a EU Council Decision, to ensure legality and compliance with the Treaties and the rules of proceedings.

The EU and restrictive measures. The European Union has an extensive use of restrictive measures that became a central tool of the Union's external action especially since the 1990s. Restrictive measures are flexible tools that allow rapid decision and enforcement (around one month) that better fit political timing and constraints. Moreover, sanctions allow better targeting to avoid the abovementioned side effects on civil populations or potential negative consequences for the Union's commerce or interests. Finally, and considering the reluctance of some Member States to conduct military action outside of the European Union (or their lack of capacity), restrictive measures are one of the few tools that provide tangible action while being cost efficient in a complex budgetary environment.

The European Union implemented all recent United Nations' Security Council embargoes, but also decided independent ones, for example against China,[10] Bosnia Herzegovina,[11] Egypt,[12] Myanmar,[13] and several other countries. The scope of sanctions decided by the European Union, although quite similar to United Nations' coercive actions, often adds travel bans in addition to the classic arms embargoes, economic sanctions and financial sanctions.

The other specificity of EU sanctions lies in the ability of blacklisted natural or legal entities to contest the legal grounds of their listing on sanction lists and obtain their removal from the EU Court of Justice, which could potentially hamper the efficiency of the considered restrictive measure. This jurisdictional impact of the EU Court of Justice over the effectiveness of sanctions is one of the growing challenges that will face the European Union's international sanctions framework. Financial sanctions may also prove difficult to enforce. They need careful and extensive regulation and close cooperation with international banks as well as non-EU countries. Considering the potential lack of cooperation of certain countries, especially for sanctions not decided by the UNSC, such measures are easily escaped.

---

[10]Declaration of the European Council in Madrid, 27 June 1989.

[11]Since 1991, cf. Council Decision 2011/173/CFSP of 22 March 2011, Official Journal of the European Union L76, p. 68.

[12]Since 2011, cf. Council Decision 2011/172/CFSP of 22 March 2011, Official Journal of the European Union L76, p. 63.

[13]Since 1991, cf. Council Decision 2013/184/CFSP of 22 April 2013, Official Journal of the European Union L111, p. 75.

Correct and coordinated implementation of EU sanctions is another growing topic within the EU. Member States' are responsible for the implementation and enforcement of EU embargoes and their interpretation of the EU Council Decision may vary regarding the scope of the sanctions or the implementation of catch-all clauses allowing the controlling of purely civil goods when they may be diverted for a military end-use in an embargoed country. The lack of a level playing field with non-EU based companies, and potentially with EU companies depending on national interpretation, is a challenge that the EU will need to tackle in the near future in order not to hamper the EU economy in difficult times, especially when sanctions decided by the EU Council may backfire on EU industries as has been the case with Russia: the EU aerospace industry raised concerns to their national authorities given that more than 50% of their supplies of titanium[14] came either from Crimea or from Russia.

2.5 Focus on the Extra-Territorial Application of U.S. Embargoes

While the European Union's decisions regarding the implementation of sanctions regimes are applicable to all EU member States, the United States policy relating to embargoes tends to establish an extra-territorial application of U.S. regulations. The United States enforces various sanctions regimes: military sanctions under the International Traffic in Arms Regulations (ITAR),[15] commercial sanctions and end-use or end-user based controls under the Export Administration Regulations (EAR),[16] and financial sanctions under various sanction programmes administrated by the Department of the Treasury, Office of Foreign Assets Control (DoT/OFAC).

U.S. international sanctions apply as soon—and as long—as there is a nexus with U.S. jurisdiction. Regarding military items, all ITAR-controlled items exported from the United States are controlled under the ITAR and thus subject to a prior authorisation from the U.S. authorities. However, once exported, either for stocking purposes or for integration into a higher assembly, and ultimately into the final product, the ITAR-controlled commodity remains subject to an export

[14]Titanium is often alloyed with iron, aluminium or other metals to produce a strong and light-weight alloy for aerospace applications (jet engines, airframe, spacecraft, etc.), as well as for several other industrial, medical and high-tech applications.

[15]The ITAR (22 C.F.R. Part 120) is the military export control regime established in the U.S. pursuant to the Arms Export Control Act of 1976 (22 U.S.C. ch. 39). The interpretation and enforcement of ITAR is under the responsibility of the Department of State, Directorate of Defence Trade Controls (DoS/DDTC).

[16]The EAR (15 C.F.R. Part 730 and following) is the dual-use export control regime established in the U.S. pursuant to the Export Administration Act of 1979 (50 U.S.C. Ch. Appendix—Export Regulation). The interpretation and enforcement of the EAR is under the responsibility of the Department of Commerce, Bureau of Industry and Security (DoC/BIS).

authorisation, regardless of its incorporated state. This means that all foreign persons that will be involved in the manufacturing, exportation and financing of the utilisation of a foreign-made product incorporating a U.S.-origin ITAR-controlled component will need prior vetting from the U.S. authorities. Should an ITAR controlled item be exported to a non-vetted foreign person (or country), the United States will consider this as a breach of U.S. regulations and the concerned entities, including foreign nationals or foreign-owned legal entities, may face prosecution in the U.S. The principle is quite similar regarding dual-use goods controlled under the EAR, although the U.S. considers that foreign-made items incorporating less than a certain amount of U.S.-controlled dual-use items are not subject to U.S. jurisdiction.[17]

As a consequence, the export of such items to a country subject to a U.S. embargo[18] is prohibited either when occurring from the U.S., or occurring outside of the U.S. but involving U.S. products, even when they are incorporated. Several companies (U.S.-based or foreign ones) have been prosecuted in the past for violating U.S. regulations and most of them finally agreed to pay heavy fines or to enter into a Consent Agreement with the U.S. authorities. Sanctions for not complying with U.S. embargoes may result in fines, debarment from export privileges in the U.S. (including re-export authorisations), imprisonment, and potentially blacklisting (and therefore the impossibility for the blacklisted company to enter into any business in the U.S. or with a U.S. national or U.S. entity).

U.S. financial sanctions necessitate a legislative act or an executive order to implement new sanctions. They are similar to the ITAR and EAR in their philosophy and enforcement methods, including extra-territorial application and potential violations from non-U.S. persons any time there is a nexus with the U.S. financial system. As a consequence, any operation involving a U.S. person (including for financing, banking, insurance, etc.) or using the U.S. currency may fall under U.S. jurisdiction.[19] The Office of Foreign Assets Control is also responsible for enforcing U.S. financial sanctions and more and more U.S. and foreign persons are being prosecuted, with an increased number of cases since the 2000s.

Such extraterritoriality of the U.S. regulations has been widely criticized in the past, including by the European Union in its EU Council Regulation No. 2271/96 of 22 November 1996[20]: 'extra-territorial application of such law, regulation and other legislative instruments violate international law' and 'may have adverse effects on the interests' of the European Union. However, even if this Regulation provides

---

[17]Cf. Export Administration Regulations Part 734.4 *de minimis*. This threshold is 25% of the fair market price value for all countries but only 10% for Cuba, Syria, Sudan, North Korea and Iran.

[18]Countries under U.S. embargo are listed in the ITAR Part 126.1 *embargoed countries*.

[19]For several examples cf. the Comprehensive Iran Sanctions, Accountability, and Divestment Act of 2010 (CISADA—PL 111-195 of 1 July 2010), the Iranian Transactions and Sanctions Regulations (ITSR—31 C.F.R Part 560), or the Cuban Liberty and Democratic Solidarity Act of 1996 (PL 104-114 of 12 March 1996).

[20]EU Council Regulation (EC) No. 2271/96 of 22 November 1996, Official Journal of the European Union L309, p. 01.

protection against the extra-territorial application of several laws, including the U.S. embargo against Cuba, its effectiveness and applicability are very limited and has not prevented several major EU companies from being prosecuted by U.S. authorities and entering into Consent Agreements without any formal diplomatic protest from their home countries. Article 4 of the Regulation however states that 'No judgment of a court or tribunal and no decision of an administrative authority located outside the Community giving effect, directly or indirectly, to the laws specified in the annex [a list laws considered as having extra-territorial application] or to actions based thereon or resulting there from, shall be recognized or be enforceable in any manner', but no country seems to have filed a formal complaint.

2.6 Embargoes and International Firms—The Challenge of Export Compliance

International sanctions decided by an assembly of states such as the United Nations or the European Union, or decided and implemented by a particular country, are essential in the conduct of international relations and the maintaining of peace by allowing coercive measures without the use of armed force and therefore reducing the threat of armed conflicts in the world.

However, their implementation and effectiveness have always been a challenge and will continue to remain so, especially considering the growing use of the Internet, the globalisation of the digital economy worldwide, the rapid increase of international exchanges of goods (either by land, by sea or by air) and the growing security challenges posed by low-intensity conflicts and global terrorism all around the globe.

Compliance with such sanctions by individuals and companies, under the global survey of their home countries' national administrations as well as public opinion and Non-Governmental Organisations is an essential element of an ethical and responsible global trade. However, and despite increasing resources allocated to compliance in large companies with a worldwide footprint, the issue of compliance is far from being properly addressed. The overall complexity of sanctions regimes is one of the reasons why countries companies are struggling to enforce these sanctions regimes.

Some of the difficulties for a company when it comes to compliance with sanctions regimes are the following:

- Combination of different sanctions regimes—United Nations, European Union, national sanctions or restrictions—against the same country or target, therefore increasing the number of legal requirements to comply with;
- Diverging scope and interpretation of sanctions regimes implemented at a supra-national level, especially within the European Union, therefore resulting in the lack of a level playing field and different interpretations depending on the country (and creating an incentive for forum shopping);

- Evolving regulations and sanctions scope depending on political and diplomatic contingencies. Such evolutions are positive and necessary in order to minimize as much as possible the negative impact for civil populations, or to escalate diplomatic pressure on the target, but creates a lack of legal certainty and a more difficult implementation in industry, including in contractual clauses in sectors with relationships that can last ten years or more, as for the aerospace industry.

In order to better harmonize the implementation and enforcement of international sanctions and to ensure compliance by the private sector and civil opinion, there is a real need for more cooperation between countries, the United Nations and the private sector. These stakeholders need to be better involved in the drafting, elaboration and monitoring of international sanctions. Private sector initiatives following UNSC Resolution 1540 (2004) such as the Botticelli Project are an essential first step; in addition, deeper mutual understanding will be key in the future for enhanced effectiveness of sanctions regimes and—in the end—preservation of international peace.

Chapter 3
The Role of the Security Council in WMD-Related Export Control: Synergy Between Resolution 1540 (2004) and Sanctions Resolutions

Masahiko Asada

Abstract This article analyzes the question of weapons of mass destruction (WMD)-related export control from a perspective of synergy between Security Council Resolution 1540 (2004) and its sanctions resolutions. Resolution 1540 (2004) has made the hitherto non-binding export control rules of the existing export control regimes legally binding on all UN member States. However, it does not include control lists with which States would implement their national export control legislation in a more harmonious manner. Sanctions resolutions of the Security Council seem to have eliminated this defect by incorporating such control lists as part of their sanctions regimes binding on all UN members. Thus, Resolution 1540 (2004) and sanctions resolutions have contributed to an effective implementation of WMD-related export control.

Keywords Security Council · Resolution 1540 (2004) · Sanctions · WMD Export control

3.1 Introduction

Export control is a tool designed to regulate the export of materials and technologies that are essential to or otherwise important in developing or producing weapons of mass destruction (WMD) or other advanced weapons systems. There are currently four regimes instituted for such purposes: the Nuclear Suppliers Group

The author acknowledges with appreciation that the research on which this article is based has been funded by the Japan Society for the Promotion of Science (2012–2016).

M. Asada (✉)
Graduate School of Law, Kyoto University, Kyoto, Japan
e-mail: asada@law.kyoto-u.ac.jp

D. Tamada and P. Achilleas (eds.), *Theory and Practice of Export Control*,
Kobe University Social Science Research Series,
DOI 10.1007/978-981-10-5960-5_3

(NSG) established in 1975,[1] the Australia Group (AG) established in 1985,[2] the Missile Technology Control Regime (MTCR) established in 1987,[3] and the Wassenaar Arrangement (WA) established in 1996.[4]

There are certain common features in these regimes. First, the way in which they operate is that the member states of the regime agree on common guidelines as well as lists for implementing the guidelines (sometimes called a "trigger list"). In the case of the NSG, for instance, two sets of guidelines govern nuclear and nuclear-related exports, respectively. Each set of NSG guidelines has an annex listing the items, technologies and software subject to the guidelines.

A second common feature of the export control regimes is that member states regularly meet to exchange information regarding proliferation concerns in the relevant areas, as well as to discuss and agree on any necessity to revise the guidelines or lists. The information exchange is no less important than the guidelines and lists themselves in implementing export control; the exchanged information often relates to procurement and denial cases that are vitally important to share with other members.

Thirdly, the four export control regimes are all so-called informal ("gentlemen's") agreements, which means they are not legally binding. It has sometimes been suggested that export control regimes should be made legally binding,[5] but there is no move in that direction so far.

Fourthly, the number of member states of the four existing regimes is relatively small, around forty: more precisely, the NSG has forty-eight member states, the AG has forty-two, the MTCR has thirty-four, and the WA has forty-one. The reason for such relatively sparse participation in export control regimes is not only that suppliers of the relevant items are relatively limited, but is also related to the concern that information sharing may adversely affect non-proliferation endeavors if participants come to include states with potential for proliferation, either active or passive.

Some of the above elements not only describe common features but may also be seen as including common shortcomings of the existing export control regimes. What has been pointed out among the most salient shortcomings of these regimes is that none of them are legally binding and that their membership is rather limited. This article addresses these aspects of the export control regimes and discusses the potential of relevant United Nations Security Council resolutions, including sanctions resolutions, for effectively rectifying these shortcomings.

[1]http://www.nuclearsuppliersgroup.org/en/ accessed 6 December 2015.

[2]http://www.australiagroup.net/en/ accessed 6 December 2015.

[3]http://www.mtcr.info/english/ accessed 6 December 2015.

[4]http://www.wassenaar.org/ accessed 6 December 2015.

[5]Takehiko Yamamoto, "Kokomu Kyotei ha Kokusaikyotei ni seyo [Make the COCOM Agreement an International Treaty]," *Sentaku*, March 1990, p. 130.

3.2 Shortcomings of the Existing Export Control Regimes

That the existing export control regimes are not legally binding means that their members are not legally obligated to implement the rules embodied in their guidelines. As a result, conduct that is apparently in contravention of the guidelines may not lead to the invocation of responsibility of the possible wrongdoer. Nor is there any formal mechanism instituted in the existing regimes for the purpose of settling compliance-related disputes. The question of the Chinese provision of nuclear reactors to Pakistan is one of the recent representative disputes in the NSG.

According to the NSG guidelines, the participating governments have agreed that:

> Suppliers should transfer *trigger list items* or related technology to a non-nuclear weapon State only when the receiving State has brought into force an agreement with the IAEA [International Atomic Energy Agency] requiring the application of safeguards on all source and special fissionable material in its current and future peaceful activities. [6] (emphasis added)

Nuclear reactors are listed as one of the trigger list items in the guidelines[7] and thus cannot be supplied to non-nuclear-weapon states that have not concluded a comprehensive safeguards agreement with the IAEA, including Pakistan and other nonparties to the Nuclear Non-Proliferation Treaty (NPT).[8] However, there is a so-called "grandfather" provision in the NSG guidelines under which suppliers may supply trigger list items to non-NPT parties. The grandfather provision provides that the stated policy "does not apply to agreements or contracts drawn up on or prior to April 3, 1992 [the date of introduction of the above rule]."[9]

When China joined the NSG in 2004, it had already built a power reactor at Pakistan's Chashma site and claimed that, under the grandfather provision, it was entitled to build a second one, on the ground that the second project was covered in its existing agreement with Pakistan.

However, it was subsequently reported that China reached a deal to sell two additional nuclear reactors to Pakistan. At the time of joining the NSG, China made a declaration covering the two Chashma reactors but not any additional plants.[10]

---

[6]IAEA Doc INFCIRC/254/Rev.12/Part 1, 13 November 2013, para. 4 (a).

[7]Ibid., Annex A, para. 2.1.

[8]Parties to the NPT are obligated to conclude a comprehensive safeguards agreement with the IAEA under Article III of the Treaty. Most of the non-nuclear-weapon states which are parties to the NPT have concluded such an agreement, but there are twelve that as yet have not. See https://www.iaea.org/sites/default/files/sg_-agreements-status-list-20-july-2015.pdf accessed 6 December 2015.

[9]IAEA Doc INFCIRC/254/Rev.12/Part 1, op. cit., para. 4 (d).

[10]Daniel Horner, "China, Pakistan Set Reactor Deal," *Arms Control Today*, Vol. 40, No. 5 (June 2010), p. 41. See also Salman Masood and Chris Buckley, "Pakistan Breaks Ground on Nuclear Plant Project with China," *New York Times*, 26 November 2013. For the controversy over China's invocation of the grandfather provision of the NSG guidelines, see "Lessons from China's Successful NSG Campaign," *Arms Control Today*, Vol. 34, No. 8 (October 2004), p. 24.

The NSG guidelines contain no justification other than resorting to the grandfather provision. Since contracts as a rule are not expected to be made public, it is quite difficult for other participating governments to disprove the Chinese claim. If the NSG regime were a hard law system with an appropriate dispute settlement mechanism, this case could be brought to such mechanism and the authenticity of the relevant documents would be checked by the competent body.

Another major shortcoming of the existing export control regimes is their limited membership. The event most dramatically showing that this is a serious shortcoming is the exposure of the nuclear trading network of Abdul Qadeer Khan (A.Q. Khan), the father of Pakistan's nuclear bomb.

The story is as follows. In December 2001, Gulf Technical Industries, a trading company set up in Dubai, United Arab Emirates (UAE), signed a contract to order centrifuge parts from Scomi Precision Engineering, a machine manufacturer in Malaysia. Centrifuges are metal tubes that spin uranium hexafluoride gas to enrich uranium by increasing the proportion of uranium 235. If the uranium is enriched to the point where uranium 235 constitutes more than 90%, it may be used for manufacturing a nuclear bomb. If it is around 3–5%, it will be used to generate electricity in a nuclear reactor. Thus, centrifuge is a typical dual-use item. In August 2003, as part of the implementation of the contract, centrifuge parts were delivered to Dubai, where they were loaded onto a German ship, the *BBC China*, bound for Libya. As the *BBC China* headed through the Suez Canal, it was intercepted by German and Italian authorities and taken to an Italian port where the parts were confiscated. It is well known that this seizure led Libya to completely give up its nuclear program.[11]

In the nuclear black market led by A.Q. Khan of Pakistan, Malaysia became the production point for centrifuge parts; and Dubai became a central transfer point.[12] Although two of the three named states (Malaysia and the UAE) are parties to the NPT, the NPT does not prohibit the transfer of centrifuges or centrifuge parts as long as they are for peaceful uses. Also, and importantly in our context, none of these three states are members of the NSG, and their nationals and companies played a pivotal role in running the nuclear black market. This fact seems to demonstrate how important it is for the NSG "rules," if not the regime itself, to cover all states with nuclear-related industries and important transit/transshipment points.

---

[11]See, e.g., William J. Broad, David E. Sanger and Raymond Bonner, "A Tale of Nuclear Proliferation: How Pakistani Built His Network," *New York Times*, 12 February 2004; "On the Trail of the Black Market Bombs," *BBC News*, 12 February 2004.

[12]David E. Sanger, "The Khan Network," paper presented at the Conference on South Asia and the Nuclear Future held June 4-5, 2004 at Stanford University, p. 2.

3.3 Security Council Resolution 1540 (2004)

3.3.1 Achievements of the Resolution

In the year following the seizure of the *BBC China*, a major achievement was accomplished in terms of making WMD export control a legal obligation: the adoption of Security Council Resolution 1540 (2004).

Resolution 1540 (2004) is a direct reaction to the 9/11 terrorist attacks and the ensuing anthrax incident taking place in the United States in 2001, which seem to have shown that "[t]he gravest danger … lies at the crossroads of radicalism and technology," using the words from the *National Security Strategy of the United States of America 2002*.[13] Thus, there was a paradigm shift in threat perception about the destination of WMD proliferation from the so-called "rogue" states to terrorists or other non-state actors.

After undergoing several revisions during the drafting stage, Resolution 1540 (2004) was adopted unanimously by the Security Council on 28 April 2004. Its main thrust is to obligate the UN member states to:

> adopt and enforce appropriate effective laws which prohibit any non-State actor to manufacture, acquire, possess, develop, transport, transfer or use nuclear, chemical or biological weapons and their means of delivery, in particular for terrorist purposes.[14]

In the export control context, the resolution also obligates the UN member states[15] to:

> take and enforce effective measures to establish domestic controls to prevent the proliferation of nuclear, chemical or biological weapons and their means of delivery, including by establishing appropriate controls over related materials and to this end, … [e]stablish, develop, review and maintain appropriate effective national export and trans-shipment controls over such items, including appropriate laws and regulations to control export, transit, trans-shipment and re-export and controls on providing funds and services related to such export and trans-shipment such as financing, and transporting that would contribute to proliferation, as well as establishing end-user controls; and establishing and enforcing appropriate criminal or civil penalties for violations of such export control laws and regulations.[16]

From our perspective, the second set of measures is of particular importance, as it refers specifically to export control. These measures are all adopted as a "decision" of the Security Council under Chapter VII of the UN Charter, meaning that they are legally binding on all UN member states.

---

[13]President George W. Bush, preface to *The National Security Strategy of the United States of America* (White House, September 2002).

[14]UN Doc S/RES/1540(2004), 28 April 2004, para. 2.

[15]The resolution itself states that "all States" shall take such and such measures, but, strictly legally speaking, it is not possible in principle for a UN resolution to impose legal obligations on non-UN-member states.

[16]UN Doc S/RES/1540(2004), op. cit., para. 3.

Thus, the Security Council, by adopting Resolution 1540 (2004), achieved what the existing export control regimes had not been able to achieve. First, the resolution imposed legally binding obligations to implement export control rules, which had hitherto been no more than guidelines.

Second, the resolution imposed these obligations on all UN member states. Until then, the guidelines were applicable only to the members of the respective export control regimes, which in number are forty, more or less. As has already been pointed out, the membership of the existing export control regimes has been deliberately limited in order, for one thing, not to disclose sensitive information to states about which there is a proliferation concern. At the same time, it is also imperative for an export control regime to cover all capable states and, preferably, all states with important transit and transshipment ports, such as Dubai. Otherwise, sensitive items may easily proliferate from or through those states. The Security Council accomplished the difficult task of obligating all UN member states to implement export control "rules" without risking the disclosure of sensitive proliferation-related *technological* information to those states that should not have access to it and also without allowing them to share sensitive proliferation-related *political* information.

In addition, the resolution went beyond the traditional export control measures at that time by covering some perceived loopholes in the existing regimes, such as lack of controls over transit and transshipment, as well as over funds and services related to such export and transshipment.[17]

3.3.2 Defects of the Resolution

This by no means signifies that Resolution 1540 (2004) is without defects; there are in fact a couple of defects in it. First, while the resolution was successful in imposing legal obligations on UN members, it did not specify the deadline by which the obligations have to be fulfilled. As a result, technically, no UN member would be held in breach of the obligations even if the obligations are not fulfilled at one point in time. Although it would have been unrealistic to give specific deadlines for the implementation of Resolution 1540 measures, considering that states vary widely in development of national export control systems, this fact nevertheless has made the 1540 obligations relatively weak.

---

[17]The existing export control regimes have seen the lack of control over brokering and transit/transshipment as a sort of loophole, and quite recently, some of them have sought to regulate those activities. The NSG's 2014 plenary meeting (held in June 2014) adopted a document titled "Good Practices for the Implementation of Brokering and Transit/Transshipment Controls"; and the Wassenaar Arrangement's 2015 plenary meeting (held in December 2015) adopted a document titled "Best Practice Guidelines for Transit or Transshipment." http://www.nuclearsuppliersgroup.org/images/Files/National_Practices/National_Good_Practices.pdf; http://www.wassenaar.org/best-practice-guidelines-for-transit-or-transshipment/ accessed 13 January 2016.

It is worth noting in this context that the Security Council set up a mechanism to facilitate the implementation of the resolution. In accordance with the decision contained in the resolution, a committee of the Security Council, called the "1540 Committee," was established. States are called upon to present a report to the committee on "steps they have taken or intend to take to implement [the] resolution." The committee then examines those reports with the support of a group of experts (currently composed of nine members) and reports to the Security Council on the implementation of the resolution.[18]

A second defect of Resolution 1540 (2004) is that the measures imposed are not specific enough to be practically effective. The resolution simply states that all states shall establish "*appropriate* effective national export and trans-shipment controls," including "*appropriate* laws and regulations to control export, transit, trans-shipment and re-export," as well as "*appropriate* criminal or civil penalties for violations of such export control laws and regulations" (emphasis added). No more detailed elaboration is made except that such measures cover controls over related funds and services and require end-user controls. It has been pointed out that most developing countries with little experience in export control would have no idea about what they are expected to do with regard to the national legislation they are legally obligated to enact.[19]

What is more, with such a loose obligation, so to speak, it is possible that a state may be considered to have fulfilled such and such parts of the 1540 obligations once it enacts legislation covering the areas referred to in the resolution, irrespective of the content of the relevant laws and regulations.

In fact, the 1540 Committee's work method appears to be along a similar line. The committee has used a matrix (called the "1540 Matrix") as the primary tool to organize information about implementation of the resolution by UN member states. In each field in the matrix, the committee denotes one of three possible responses, "X," "?" and blank. Of these, it is said that even "X," the highest mark, does not indicate that the measures taken fully implement an obligation under Resolution 1540 (2004); rather, it only indicates that the 1540 Committee and its experts have found "evidence that the State has taken a measure or measures relevant to a particular field."[20]

Third, Resolution 1540 (2004) does not include an important element for any export control system to operate effectively, i.e., control lists. Indeed, agreeing on lists and on their revisions is one of the most important tasks of the meetings of the existing export control regimes. It is not an exaggeration to say that no export control regime can function well without a control list.

---

[18]UN Doc S/RES/1540(2004), op. cit., para. 4.

[19]Laurence Scheinman and Johan Bergenas (2010) "UN Security Council Resolution 1540," *CISTEC Journal*, No. 126 (March 2010), p. 13.

[20]"The 1540 Matrix." http://www.un.org/en/sc/1540/national-implementation/matrix.shtml accessed 6 December 2015.

Admittedly, in a footnote to Resolution 1540 (2004), a definition is given for the key term of "related materials" as the objects of 1540 export control. The term is defined as:

> materials, equipment and technology covered by relevant *multilateral treaties and arrangements*, or included on *national control lists*, which could be used for the design, development, production or use of nuclear, chemical and biological weapons and their means of delivery. (emphasis added)

However, there is no such list in multilateral WMD non-proliferation "treaties" except for the Chemical Weapons Convention.[21] Multilateral "arrangements" appears to refer to the existing export control regimes, but their membership is limited as pointed out earlier. "National control lists" are only available in such states as have already been engaged in export controls, and not in states where it is hoped they will be introduced. Thus, the definition of "related materials" in Resolution 1540 (2004) does not really serve its hoped-for purposes. In this respect, special attention should be paid to the important role that UN sanctions resolutions have played.

3.4 UN Sanctions Resolutions

The United Nations has a long history of imposing sanctions on its members as well as on others under Chapter VII of the UN Charter. However, imposing sanctions for WMD non-proliferation purposes is a relatively recent phenomenon.[22] The first such move took place in July 2006 when the Security Council imposed economic sanctions on North Korea in response to the latter's launch of ballistic missiles. The Security Council in Resolution 1695 (2006) "require[d]":

> all Member States, in accordance with their national legal authorities and legislation and consistent with international law, to … prevent missile and missile-related items, materials, goods and technology being transferred to DPRK's missile or WMD programmes.

Of the items subject to the embargo, missiles are not difficult to identify, while missile-*related* items, materials, goods and technology are. The problem of identifying the latter was soon rectified by the ensuing resolutions on North Korea.

[21] See CWC, Annex on Chemicals, Schedule of Chemicals. The Zangger Committee has produced a list of items for export control under Article III, paragraph 2, of the NPT (called the Zangger List). IAEA Doc INFCIRC/209/Rev.3, June 2014. However, this committee is not a formal, NPT-based group with a mandate to produce a list of items relevant to the said paragraph. See http://www.foi.se/en/Customer–Partners/Projects/zc/zangger/ accessed 6 December 2015.

[22] One of the reasons for the change seems to be that the Security Council's concept of "threat to the peace" against which it can take enforcement action has been broadened to include the proliferation of weapons of mass destruction with the issuance of its Presidential Statement in January 1992.

The Security Council, in Resolution 1718 (2006) adopted in October 2006 in response to the first North Korean nuclear test, "decide[d]" under Chapter VII of the UN Charter that:

> [a]ll Member States shall prevent the direct or indirect supply, sale or transfer to the DPRK [Democratic People's Republic of Korea], through their territories or by their nationals, or using their flag vessels or aircraft, and whether or not originating in their territories, of … [a]ll items, materials, equipment, goods and technology *as set out in the lists* in documents S/2006/814 and S/2006/815, unless within 14 days of adoption of this resolution the Committee has amended or completed their provisions also taking into account the list in document S/2006/816 … (emphasis added)

Security Council documents S/2006/814, S/2006/815, and S/2006/816 mentioned in the Resolution contain lists reproduced from those of the NSG, MTCR, and AG, respectively.[23]

This resolution is noteworthy in many respects. First, it clearly imposes on all UN member states a legally binding obligation to prevent the transfer of the said items, materials, etc., to the DPRK by using the verb "decide" in the operative paragraph. Secondly, that obligation is quite comprehensive in terms of the mode of transfer, covering not only direct but also indirect transfers (via third states), as well as transfers not only through the territories of member states but also by their nationals or using their flag vessels or aircraft, and whether or not originating in their territory. However, the most important aspect of the resolution's embargo system seems to lie in the fact that it specifies the items, materials, equipment, goods, and technology by using lists of existing export control regimes. The importance of the existence of lists in implementing embargoes and export controls cannot be exaggerated too much.

In the Security Council, however, using lists of existing export control regimes should not have been as easy as it may appear: as pointed out earlier, the membership of the existing regimes is rather limited, and even a permanent member of the Security Council may not be a member. For example, China is neither a member of the AG nor one of the MTCR.[24] A non-member of an export control regime may well oppose using lists of the regimes of which it is not a member. If that state is a permanent member of the Security Council, such opposition means a veto. That is perhaps why, in relation to Resolution 1540 (2004), the Security Council developed its own documents that are different from the lists of the export control regimes, at least in form. The end result, however, was not different from using the regimes' lists themselves, since the Security Council documents are reproductions of the existing export control regimes' lists.

---

[23]Resolution 1737 (2006), imposing sanctions on Iran, also used Security Council documents S/2006/814 and S/2006/815 (lists of the NSG and MTCR) with certain modifications. UN Doc S/RES/1737(2006), 23 December 2006, paras. 3–7.

[24]For the background of China not being admitted to the MTCR, for example, see Victor Zaborsky, "Does China Belong in the Missile Technology Control Regime?," *Arms Control Today*, Vol. 34, No. 8 (October 2004), pp. 20–26; Wade Boese, "Missile Regime Puts Off China," *Arms Control Today*, Vol. 34, No. 9 (November 2004), p. 39.

3.5 Relations Between Export Control and Sanctions: Possible Synergy

There is an argument by some states, such as Russia, that export control should not be confused with sanctions because they are completely different systems. It is true that embargo as a sanction is placed against a specific target state whereas export control is a system to be applied to all states in principle. However, in terms of what is to be done nationally, there is no big difference between export controls under the existing export control regimes and UN-sponsored sanctions. In fact, UN sanctions are implemented in Japan, for instance, by applying the existing legislation on export control (the Foreign Exchange and Foreign Trade Control Law).

That being so, a state that has no national export control system in place has to develop and institute one if a UN-mandated sanction requires all UN members to impose an embargo, whichever state is the target. If such a state establishes the necessary system, that system could also be used, beyond that specific sanction, for export control in general by simply changing the target from a specific state to all states. What is crucial is to institute a national export control system, for whatever reasons. From a practical point of view—despite what is said above about the importance of control lists—the existence of such a system is more important than that of lists to be used for control, because various lists are publicly available and all a state is required to do after establishing a system is to decide to use them in whole or in part. In that sense, it makes little difference whether a state is legally obligated to introduce a control system by Security Council Resolution 1540 (2004) or by a UN-mandated sanctions resolution.

Enacting national export control legislation is important even without intelligence or inspection capabilities to locate or detect the presence of proliferation-related items on board. Assume that the United States detects, in a port of another state, a ship whose cargo is believed to contain items the export of which is prohibited by a Security Council resolution. If that other state does not have relevant legislation, it cannot do anything about it. On the contrary, if it has, the state can inspect the vessel and the cargo and seize the prohibited items if it finds them. Considering that many inspection activities thus far have been based on intelligence provided by other states such as the United States, the importance of a state having the legal authority to conduct an inspection and seize items cannot be exaggerated. In this connection, the wide scope of the measures mandated by Resolution 1540 (2004) should also be noted: they are supposed to cover not only export and re-export but also transit and transshipment.

3.6 Conclusion

To conclude, some of the findings warrant summarizing. First, it has been pointed out that the shortcomings of the existing export control regimes include their non-legal nature and their limited membership, which may sometimes have led to their ineffective functioning. The limited membership is required partly because of the need to protect proliferation-related sensitive information. In this connection, Security Council Resolution 1540 (2004) has skillfully made the establishment of a national proliferation-related export control system a *legal* obligation of *all* UN member states, without any need to be worried about the risk of disclosing sensitive information.

Secondly, of course Resolution 1540 (2004) has its own defects. In particular, it does not include any list to be used for implementing export control. Without common control lists, export control may not function effectively, because if State A prohibits the export of a certain item but State B does not, all the proliferator need do is to approach State B. This shortcoming of the absence of lists was remedied by Security Council sanctions resolutions, including Resolution 1718 (2006) imposing mandatory sanctions against North Korea. In that resolution, the Security Council used documents that reproduced lists of existing export control regimes as its own lists for embargoes imposed against North Korea, thereby effectively making the export control regimes' control lists legally binding on all UN member states. Thus, through Resolution 1540 (2004) and sanctions resolutions, establishing a national export control system with common control lists has become a legal obligation for all UN member states.

A legal *obligation* to put in place a national export control system does not necessarily lead to the actual setting up of such a system. The actual, effective implementation of that obligation may require some practical arrangements, including an arrangement for information gathering and assessment regarding implementation, as well as a system to provide assistance to those states that need it. In that sense, too, both Resolution 1540 (2004) and sanctions resolutions are expected to play a crucial role. They are equipped with a group (or panel) of experts who conduct an expert analysis of information provided by member states regarding the implementation of the relevant resolutions. Resolution 1540 (2004) also invites states in a position to do so to offer assistance to those states that lack the legal and regulatory infrastructure, implementation experience, and resources.[25]

All of this seems to suggest that there is a possibility of effective synergy between Resolution 1540 (2004) and sanctions resolutions of the Security Council.

References

Broad, William J., David E. Sanger, and Raymond Bonner. 2004. A Tale of Nuclear Proliferation: How Pakistani Built His Network. *New York Times*, Feb 12.

Horner, Daniel. 2010. China, Pakistan Set Reactor Deal. *Arms Control Today*, 40(5): 41 Jun.

Masood, Salman, and Chris Buckley. 2013. Pakistan Breaks Ground on Nuclear Plant Project with China. *New York Times*, Nov 26.

[25]S/RES/1540 (2004), op. cit., para. 7.

Sanger, David E. 2004. The Khan Network. Paper presented at the Conference on South Asia and the Nuclear Future, held at Stanford University, June 4–5.

Scheinman, Laurence, and Johan Bergenas. 2010. UN Security Council Resolution 1540. *CISTEC Journal*, (126): 11 Mar.

Part II
Implementing Export Control in Business Scene

Chapter 4
Export Control in Japan and CISTEC

Hisashi Riko

Abstract This article is intended to introduce Export Control in Japan briefly explaining from its unique Historical Background, Administrative Authority, Legal Framework, Control System, Licensing System. This article also focuses functions of CISTEC by referring their activities as to Committee Activities, various services for exporters etc. and how they have realized good communication among Industry, Government and Academia on Export Control and eventually high level of awareness in Japan.

Keywords Export control in japan · CISTEC

4.1 Historical Background

Japan's export control system was founded back in 1949 when the country was still under the Allied Occupation. Stepping forward into the post-World War II recovery, the Japanese government introduced that year the Foreign Exchange and Foreign Trade Control Act, which was enacted to control foreign exchange and foreign trade transactions, and which is still the basic law that governs export controls in Japan.

Three years later in 1952, Japan joined COCOM, the Coordination Committee for Multilateral Export Controls, and started implementing export controls within the framework of the multilateral export control regime that was started in 1949 and ended in 1994 after the end of the Cold War.

Much later in 1987, the basis of Japan's present day export control system was established. This development was in fact a consequence of the so-called Toshiba Machinery Incident, which involved exports of state-of-the-art machine tools from Japan to the Soviet Union The disclosure of these exports created an international uproar, especially in Washington, D.C., that this transfer of technology, a violation

H. Riko (✉)
CISTEC, Member of the Board, Tokyo, Japan
e-mail: h-riko@cistec.or.jp

D. Tamada and P. Achilleas (eds.), *Theory and Practice of Export Control*,
Kobe University Social Science Research Series,
DOI 10.1007/978-981-10-5960-5_4

of national as well as COCOM regulations, seriously undermined Western-bloc security.

In response to this incident, the government drastically enhanced controls by amending the basic law. In order to make the system more effective, the authority not only increased the penalties, but also ordered individual companies to establish an appropriate system of corporate export controls based on an internal compliance program (ICP). Shortly after that in 1989, the organization CISTEC was created as a driving force for the sound development of export controls in Japan.

Since then Japan's export control system has been evolving in response to year-to-year changes in the political and security situations of Japan and the world. Catch-all control related to weapons of mass destruction (WMD) was introduced in 2002, brokering and transit controls were introduced in 2007 and technology transfer control was enhanced in 2009. Further, in April 2014, the government realigned its arms export control policy and set out the new Three Principles on Transfer of Defense Equipment and Technology, replacing the Three Principles on Arms Exports which had lasted for almost 50 years.

Today, Japan, as a signatory to major non-proliferation treaties and a member to all the existing international export control regimes, is implementing robust export controls consistent with the international standards and norms. In addition, Japan not only commits itself to international non-proliferation goals, but also promotes its outreach activities in Asia, expanding cooperative networks in the region.

4.2 Administrative Authority

In Japan, the Ministry of Economy, Trade and Industry (METI), originally formed in 1949, is the competent authority that administers export controls. In METI, the Security Export Control Policy Division, the Security Export Inspection Office, and the Security Export Licensing Division are the units in charge. As shown below, they are situated under the Trade Control Department of the Trade and Economic Bureau, and form a staff of about 80 officers in total.

(1) The Security Export Control Policy Division

The Security Export Control Policy Division is responsible for export control policy setting, legislation, and overall administration. It joins discussions in international export control regimes and organizes international outreach activities.

(2) The Security Export Licensing Division

The Security Export Licensing Division is responsible for examining license applications and issuing licenses. It has some one hundred officers including those in regional offices.

(3) The Security Export Inspection Office

The Security Export Inspection Office is responsible for conducting company inspections. It gives instructions and guidance to exporters and conducts domestic outreach activities.

4.3 Legal Framework

4.3.1 Legal Structure

The legal structure of Japan's export control system is extremely complicated. It is not a simple set of law and regulations, but is a complex mix of primary legislation and secondary legislation. Actually, the basic law is followed by a wide scope of subordinate regulations issued from time to time in the form of cabinet orders, ministerial ordinances, notifications, notices and guidance, which are interrelated in a complex way. Of those, the principal ones are as follows.

(1) The Foreign Exchange and Foreign Trade Act (1998) (basic law)

The Foreign Exchange and Foreign Trade Act (the Act), originally enacted in 1949, is the basic law that provides the legal basis for export controls in Japan.

(2) The Export Trade Control Order (1949) (Cabinet order)

The Export Trade Control Order specifies the controlled goods pursuant to the provisions of Article 48-(1) of the Act.

(3) The Foreign Exchange Order (1980) (Cabinet order)

The Foreign Exchange Order specifies the controlled technology including software pursuant to the provisions of Article 25-1-(1) of the Act.

4.3.2 The Foreign Exchange and Foreign Trade Act

4.3.2.1 Overview

In 1949, when Japan had just started its economic reconstruction after the war, the basic law was introduced first as the Foreign Exchange and Foreign Trade Control Act to strictly control foreign exchange and foreign trade transactions for the purpose of normalizing trade activities and maintaining Japan's balance of payments. Half-century later in 1998, when foreign exchange business was completely liberalized, it was amended and superseded by the current Foreign Exchange and Foreign Trade Act, in which the law's control implication was eliminated.

4.4 Control System

4.4.1 Overview

As stated in Article 1 of the Foreign Exchange and Foreign Trade Act, it is the policy of the Government of Japan to impose necessary as well as minimum controls on export transactions to contribute to the maintenance of national as well as international peace and security while maintaining the principle of free trade. Accordingly, the government requires a Japanese person to apply for a license when exporting specific goods to a foreign country or transferring specific technologies to a foreign person or a foreign country.

4.4.2 Transactions Subject to Control

Under the Act, the following transactions are subject to control.

(1) Export of goods
(2) Transfer of technologies
(3) Transshipment of goods
(4) Brokering transactions related to goods or technologies.

4.4.3 Control Types

Japan enforces two types of control: list control; and catch-all control.

4.4.4 List Control

4.4.4.1 Control Lists

List control is a control that is implemented by listing sensitive items (goods, technology, or software) subject to control in certain lists as part of the regulations. In Japan, controlled goods and controlled technologies, including software, are listed separately in Attachment List No. 1 to the Export Trade Control Order and in the Attachment List to the Foreign Exchange Order, respectively.

Each control list contains 16 categories of items, and those under categories 1 through 15 are controlled items subject to list control, while others under category 16 are non-controlled items but are subject to catch-all control. The items are identified by classification numbers that are specific to Japan, not according to the European numbering system which is used by the EU member nations as well as by some other countries.

The controlled items

Japanese category	Type of control	Classification of the items			International regimes
1	List control	Military items	Arms		WA/ML
2		Dual-use items	WMD-related	Nuclear items	NSG
3				Chemical weapons	AG
3-2				Biological weapons	AG
4				Missiles	MTCR
5			Conventional arms-related	Advanced materials	WA Cat. 1
6				Material processing	WA Cat. 2
7				Electronics	WA Cat. 3
8				Computers	WA Cat. 4
9				Communication/information security	WA Cat. 5
10				Sensors and lasers	WA Cat. 6
11				Navigation/avionics	WA Cat. 7
12				Marine	WA Cat. 8
13				Aerospace/propulsion	WA Cat. 9
14				Other ML items	Except for WA/ML
15				Sensitive items	WA very sensitive
16	Catch-all control	Items other than those under categories 1–15			

4.4.4.2 Export of Goods

An export of controlled goods on Attachment List No. 1 to the Export Trade Control Order requires a license issued by the Minister of Economy, Trade and Industry for all countries and regions.

4.4.4.3 Transfer of Technologies

Covered by a separate article in the Act, technology transfer in Japan is controlled in a unique manner based principally on the "residency" of the person who transfers or receives technology. Before April 2009, when the Act was amended, the rule was so simple that a transfer of controlled technology or software from a resident to a non-resident was subject to licensing. In April 2009, however, the control was rearranged and enhanced to match the present age of globalized economy in which people move freely from country to country and technology from person to person electronically.

Especially important is that a concept of border-based control was introduced in this enhancement.

The essence of the current technology transfer control is described as follows. (Hereinafter, the term "technology" is used to mean technology as well as software).

4.4.5 Catch-All Control

4.4.5.1 Background

The present style WMD catch-all control was introduced in 2002 to replace the Complementary Control. Then in 2008, the government expanded it further by introducing military catch-all control.

4.4.5.2 WMD Catch-All Control

Overview

WMD catch-all control requires exporters to obtain a license when METI orders them to do so in respect to a specific transaction ("informed" condition), or when exporters are aware that the item will be used for the development, manufacture, use, or storage of WMD, in other words, if the transaction falls under certain conditions provided objectively by the government ("objective" condition).

The scope of items subject to the control is broad. Unlike list control, any goods and technologies, including non-controlled items, are subject to WMD catch-all control, except for specific non-sensitive items such as food and timbers.

4.4.5.3 Military Catch-All Control

Overview

The two cabinet orders related to export controls were amended on August 27, 2008 to introduce control on non-controlled items for military end-use, which was effected on the first day of November of the same year. Since then Japan has been implementing catch-all control related to both WMD and conventional weapons.

4.4.6 Brokering Control

In June 2007, METI enforced regulations to control WMD-related brokering and transshipment services. Those regulations were introduced to meet the requirements of the UN Security Council Resolution 1540 adopted in April 2004. The brokering control was further enhanced in April 2009.

4.5 Transshipment Control

Transshipment control is applied to foreign goods passing through Japan. The term "transshipment" is defined as an act to transship foreign goods at airports or seaports in Japan.

(1) Transshipment of arms

Transshipment of arms under category 1 of the control list requires a license.

(2) Transshipment of goods other than arms

A person in Japan must obtain a license when transshipping goods if;

(a) The person has been so informed by METI, or
(b) The person has come to know, through written information on such documents as contracts or corporate brochures, or through notification from the importer or any other parties, that the items will be used for the development, manufacture, use or storage of WMD.

Transshipment control does not apply, however, to the transaction whose destination is Argentina, Australia, Austria, Belgium, Bulgaria, Canada, the Czech Republic, Denmark, Finland, France, Germany, Greece, Hungary, Ireland, Italy, South Korea, Luxemburg, the Netherlands, New Zealand, Norway, Poland, Portugal, Spain, Sweden, Switzerland, the U.K., or the U.S.A.

4.6 Licensing System

4.6.1 Overview

In Japan, an export license is issued only by the Minister of Economy, Trade and Industry. When necessary, exporters must submit license applications to the Security Export Licensing Division of the Trade Control Department, or to its regional office, where licensing officers examine the applications focusing on the end-use and the end-user.

4.6.2 Licensing Policy

4.6.2.1 Dual-Use Items

A license will be issued if METI has determined that the items involved will not materially contribute to the design, development, or production of WMD or conventional weapons, nor be circumvented or re-exported to countries or entities of concern.

4.6.2.2 Military Items

Overview

Japan as a peace-loving nation has traditionally been taking a very tough stance against exports of arms or anything of military significance. Such a stance first resulted in the introduction in 1967 of the guideline called the Three Principles on Arms Exports which prohibited arms exports with limited exceptions. This policy of arms export prohibition lasted until 2014, when the government set out a new guideline called the Three Principles on Transfer of Defense Equipment and Technology.

4.6.2.3 The Three Principles on Transfer of Defense Equipment and Technology

In 2014, the said policy of arms export prohibition was reviewed and realigned. This was done along with the Abe Administration's efforts to reestablish its security policy framework so that Japan can take more responsibility for the peace and stability in the world.

4.6.3 Export License

Exporters may obtain either an individual export license or a bulk export license, depending on the sensitivity and security concerns of the items and the destinations.

4.6.3.1 Individual Export License

Bulk Export License

Overview

A bulk export license simplifies the licensing procedures by allowing licensees to make multiple exports of controlled items under certain conditions related to classification, destinations, end-use, and so on. Effective on July 1, 2012, the bulk licensing system was rationalized and rearranged into the five license types, as shown in the following table.

The bulk export licenses

Category	No	Name of the licenses
General bulk license	1.	General bulk export license
Special bulk license	2.	Special general bulk export license
	3.	Special bulk export license
	4.	Special bulk export license for repair or replacement
	5.	Special bulk export license for overseas subsidiaries

4.7 Communication Between METI, CISTEC and Exporters

4.7.1 Overview

For promoting export control awareness among exporters, METI provides multiple channels that enable it, considering that keeping close communication with export control communities is essential. What is outstanding in this regard is the existence of CISTEC, an organization that functions as a linkage between the authority, industries and academia.

4.7.2 CISTEC

4.7.2.1 About CISTEC

CISTEC, the Center for Information on Security Trade Control, was founded in April 1989, shortly after Japan's export controls were drastically strengthened, as a non-profit and non-government organization; its operation is maintained by approx. 40 staff members and is supported financially and operationally by more than 400 associate members, including major exporting companies and research institutes (as of April 2015).

CISTEC's mission is to function as a linkage between the authority, industry and academia and help them create an efficient and effective system of export controls in Japan, and thereby contribute to the promotion of the peace and security of the world. CISTEC plays the roles to:

(1) Collect experts' knowledge and wisdom and apply it for the betterment of the Japanese system,
(2) Support Japanese companies and others for their establishment of appropriate internal export control systems,
(3) Develop advanced online systems for the provision of necessary information for exporters, and
(4) Promote international cooperation mainly with Asian countries to increase export control awareness and harmonization.

4.7.2.2 Main Activities

(1) Research and analysis, and proposal to METI
(2) Company support
(3) Information provision
(4) International cooperation.

4.7.2.3 Export Control Research Committee

What characterizes CISTEC most is its committee activities. Under the heading of the Export Control Research Committee, CISTEC has two research boards: the Policy, Rules and Procedures Board; and the Goods and Materials Board. These boards have various subcommittees established for specific research themes as mentioned below. Through these activities, CISTEC gathers industry opinions and consolidates them into public comments and proposals to the government.

4.7.2.4 Certification Program

Another important activity of CISTEC is its certification program. CISTEC maintains a program to grant certificates to people who have been qualified for having certain levels of knowledge about export controls. The levels of the qualification are set in three categories: STC Associate, STC Advanced and STC Expert. Encouraging people to challenge the examinations, CISTEC aims to promote their professional skills and motivate them to play a leading role as an expert in each company. Also, CISTEC expects that companies consider it as a merit of their job performance.

Chapter 5
Export Basics, Specificities and Consequences for Industry: How an International Group Can Manage Its Business with Sanctioned Countries

Arnaud Idiart

Abstract This article presents the Governmental character of Export Control which made its sensitivity and complexity. Industrial companies must comply with numerous national specificities of laws and regulations (extraterritorial for the USA) that apply in a moving international context of geopolitical and foreign policy interests. Moreover, the control of 'intangible transfers' has been put under the responsibility of exporters when at the same time export control has to face more and more powerful communication systems and networks. As of today, private companies make their best efforts to mitigate the export control risk, the practical Airbus process is presented. The conclusion proposes to trigger a common action of industry experts and academics to select and educate the future national elites of export control that faces a chronic shortfall in human resources.

Keywords Export-control · Compliance · Sanctions · End-use End-user · Intangibles, ex-post controls

5.1 Export Control Basics, Specificities, and Related Consequences for Industry

Export control laws and regulations can be traced back to distant times, at least on a domestic level. For instance, the Frankish swords' alloy and their tempering process brought a real ascendancy to the Frankish armies. For that reason, around the year 800, Emperor Carolus Magnus pronounced a ban on selling these swords outside of the empire and King Charles the Bald confirmed this with the 'Edict of Pistre in 864! However, major international regulations appeared only during the 20th century. To give a rough order of magnitude, today about $150 billion a year is the

A. Idiart (✉)
AIRBUS, Suresnes, France
e-mail: Arnaud.idiart@airbus.com

D. Tamada and P. Achilleas (eds.), *Theory and Practice of Export Control*, Kobe University Social Science Research Series,
DOI 10.1007/978-981-10-5960-5_5

average amount of licences delivered worldwide for exports of controlled goods and technology. The implementation of export control laws and regulations is increasingly heavy for both government agencies and exporting companies.

Technology improves more and more quickly, and due to its dematerialisation, it spreads like wildfire, faster and easier in more and more intangible forms. To face the increasing threats resulting in particular from asymmetric conflicts and terrorism and the soaring international trade, the harmonisation of export control is more and more important for ensuring a peaceful world. It is therefore of essence for exporting companies to ensure that they are compliant in their daily business and that the entire supply chain they work with is equally compliant as well. For non-compliant companies, damages can indeed be dramatic. In addition to the criminal sanctions and imprisonment of the executives, high fines are not unusual and the consequences for corporate image may be fatal.

From a legal standpoint, export control laws and regulations are an exception to the free trade principles that govern international commercial exchanges. Companies offering controlled goods or services need to comply with such rather complex and moving areas of the law wherever they are operating. Moreover, for export compliance purposes, companies need to consider more than export control laws and regulations, as they must also know about related or connected domains such as the following: (a) bribery in international commerce;[1] (b) arms brokering;[2] (c) allies' sanctions participation;[3] (d) exchange control and/or currency regulations; (e) tax and customs duties; (f) foreign investments; (g) disclosure of classified information (i.e., information which, if it is disclosed to a foreign person, may endanger national security);[4] and (h) anti-trust. All or part of the above mentioned domains may have to be considered for export control compliance purposes; in general, they are to be looked at more carefully in the context of military or dual-use goods exports. Especially, considerations about classified information and foreign investment laws and regulations have to be investigated since they are directly connected to the control of exports of military or dual-use goods.

---

[1]OECD Convention on Combating Bribery of Foreign Public Officials in International Business Transactions (http://www.oecd.org/document/20/0,2340,en_2649_34859_2017813_1_1_1_1,00.html) and the transposition of such convention into a number of domestic laws around the world. All 35 OECD countries participate.

[2]See, for instance on the matter, European Council Common Position n° 2003/468/CFSP 'regarding controls on armament brokering', adopted by the EU Member States on 23 June 2003 (EU OJ L 156 of 25 June 2003, p. 79).

[3]Sanctions and embargos are available actions by the Security Council acting under Chapter VII of the UN Charter, in the event of any threat to the peace, breach of the peace, or act of aggression.

[4]As an illustration, for France, information classification and protection of information, once classified, falls into the domain of national security and defence protection [*Instruction Générale Interministérielle sur la protection du Secret de Défense Nationale* n° 1300/SGDN/PSE/SSD of November 2011, 30th (https://www.legifrance.gouv.fr/affichTexte.do?cidTexte=JORFTEXT000024892134&categorieLien=id)] or national heritage protection (*Circulaire Interministérielle de Mise en Œuvre du Dispositif de Protection du Potentiel Scientifique et Technique de la Nation Circulaire SGDSN/AIST/PST_7nov2012_PPST*).

As export control matters are quite complex and, very often, of difficult implementation, they are subject to a number of misconceptions.

First, a paradox is that export control laws and regulations (such an important matter that concerns numerous goods and services in vast sectors of the economy directly impacting nations and citizen security) are not identified as an academic matter; this skill is not taught in law schools and accordingly is rather unpublicised. Indeed, a few publications exist that describe what export control is,[5] but very few law firms (US excepted) have it as a practice and can offer significant experience in this field. Therefore, it becomes more and more difficult to keep up to date and aware of how texts are interpreted and implemented. Constant changes induce a relative lack of jurisprudence due to few court judgements or published administrative decisions on these matters. Yet, as export control laws and regulations are very complex and are constantly evolving, they require experts to provide daily business with reliable guidelines and references. For companies, this increasing complexity necessitates more investments, which heightens the compliance costs. In particular, they have to appoint internal or external experts to advise them and guarantee mandatory export control compliance. This new requirement to secure the business is widening the gap between the companies that can afford to pay for such compliance and those that cannot. Finally, this impairs the competitiveness of small and medium-sized enterprises. A vast majority of SMEs cannot afford the risk of severe sanctions for non-compliance and accordingly are forced to withdraw from international competition and choose not to export controlled items.

Although the use of weapons is framed by the law and may be banned by certain texts, exports of weapons are less rarely forbidden in a general way in international treaties. Such is the case, for instance, in the United Nations Charter that prohibits the recourse to force[6] but does not address, per se, the issue of weapons commerce.[7] A frequent misconception about export controls is that they apply only to lethal war weapons and pieces of equipment. In fact, they could apply equally to a whole array of goods, technology, software, and services that sometimes are only indirectly related to military purposes. For example, civil planes may be subject to export control regulations because they may be used ultimately for military transport missions or because they may contain some potentially 'dual use' military and/or civilian equipment or technology. Indeed, breaches of laws and regulations can happen without the conscious knowledge of companies that do not pay sufficient attention to the export control question and heavy sanctions (even criminal) could apply whether or not the breach is made on purpose. Additionally, there is always a dramatic risk of degradation to a company's reputation.

---

[5]e.g.: Export Control Law and Regulations Handbook Third Edition—(Kluwer Law International/ Global Trade Law Series Volume 33) ISBN: 9789041154439—https://lrus.wolterskluwer.com/store/products/export-control-law-regulations-handbook-third-prod-9041154434/hardcover-item-1-9041154434.

[6]United Nations Charter, article 2, par. 4.

[7]See Martinez (1983); The Recent Arms Trade Tready (2013) gives a first answer to this issue.

A further public misconception is that, given the international scope of controls, applicable laws and regulations are primarily international. In fact, they are not. One of the most important issues relates to the fact that very few harmonised rules exist with respect to the export of military goods or services, and the number of examples of fully and exclusively transposed common rules in domestic legislation is very low. Additionally, national laws and regulations are very often adapted to the economic stakes and weight of national champions (nuclear, chemical, biological, military, dual-use, etc.). Due to the strong leveraging power of the arms trade in diplomatic negotiations, every country wants to maintain the highest level of sovereignty; all governments create and maintain purely national specificities. In spite of numerous attempts, the control of the commerce of weapons has never found a true base in international or regional treaties. Controls of weapons have always been the exclusive domain of states because such control provides them with one of the major attributes of their sovereignty. Surprisingly, the shortfall in human resources and governmental competencies is a quasi-constant reality that contributes to confounding the export control of sensitive products.

Nevertheless, for years nations worked together to harmonise the basics of control through International Groups such as the Wassenaar Arrangement (WA—1993-41 members today) or the Missile Technology Control Regime (MTCR—1987-35 partners today). These communities publish common export control lists, non-binding directives, licensing recommendations, and so forth. With the EU Intra-Community Transfer Directive published in 2009[8] http://eur-lex.europa.eu/LexUriServ/LexUriServ.do?uri=OJ:L:2009:146:0001:0036:en:PDF. and more recently the UN Arms Trade Treaty (ATT),[9] international institutions took a step forward in the harmonisation. The implementation of these two fundamental texts is very recent and of course, it is too early to make a global assessment of their real direct and indirect effects. Impacts are both for governments carrying out control and companies that are being controlled at the international level. With respect to dual-use goods and services harmonisation, even if globally more progress has been made, there is still a long way to go to achieve international harmonisation. It is worth mentioning here that major actors such as China, India and Israel are not members (yet) of the Wassenaar Arrangement that embraces 41 countries all over the world. Moreover, the most important international fora rely on each

[8]DIRECTIVE 2009/43/EC OF THE EUROPEAN PARLIAMENT AND OF THE COUNCIL of 6 May 2009; simplifying terms and conditions of transfers of defence-related products within the Community; Official Journal of the European Union—L 146/1-10.6.2009.

[9]Under the landmark Arms Trade Treaty (ATT), countries regulate the international trade in conventional weapons—from small arms to battle tanks, combat aircraft and warships—and work to prevent the diversion of arms and ammunition. The UN General Assembly of 2 April 2013 (71st Plenary Meeting) adopted the Arms Trade Treaty as a resolution by a 154-to-3 vote with 23 abstentions. The treaty was opened for formal signature by all states in New York on 3 June 2013. It entered into force on 24 December 2014, 90 days after the date of the 50th ratification. As of January 2017, the enforcement situation is the following: States Parties: 91; Ratifications/Accessions: 88; Signatories: 130.—https://s3.amazonaws.com/unoda-web/wp-content/uploads/2017/02/ATT-status-table-WebReport-27-Feb-2016.pdf.

government's good will, not on legally binding commitments; their interest is to provide common lists of controlled goods and technologies. Even inside the European Union, despite some harmonisation that has been achieved, there are still many enforcement discrepancies between the various member states that periodic reviews and updates have not totally ended, yet. This situation generates a lot of extra costs and administrative burdens for companies which need, whatever the price to be paid, to totally comply with export control laws in all countries.

Indeed, the complexity of export laws and regulations results not from the principles themselves but, much more, from the way the rules are set up and enforced. Export control is made of a high degree of sovereignty and other political considerations together with an important amount of diplomacy, reciprocity obligations, and from certain states, extra-territorial commitments. Export control applies to a very large number of situations. One example is information shared through electronic networks (e.g., computer servers and IT collaboration rooms [i.e., dedicated software] allowing teamwork from distant places, using the Internet or intranet technologies). As soon as such collaboration may involve controlled technical data and is accessible from persons located in foreign countries (or even foreign persons on national territory), an export license is required. Due to the evolution of networks, electronic work environments allowing engineering offices to be located in several countries, to guaranty full compliance with all of the applicable export control laws and regulations in various countries is very difficult, and a careful assessment of the potential issues has to be made daily. Technology is constantly evolving, and the increasing number of intangible transfers makes the efficiency of controls more and more difficult. The questions to be answered are basically the following: how is access to the environment controlled? How are the rights of the individuals who are supposed to access the technology granted and protected? How is it guaranteed that a person accessing the system is actually the right individual whose right of access has been regularly granted? How can communications be protected from the server to the user against surreptitious interceptions? How can integrity of information be guaranteed?

Additionally, in respect to the commerce in arms, dual-use goods, and services,[10] there are growing transparency concerns and demands. Governments are first interested; however, an increasing number of requests come from companies' stakeholders (rating agencies, shareholders, investors such as pension funds having ethical inclinations, non-governmental organisations, etc.).

Today, given the state of the development of technology in the context of rising international terrorism, export controls have become extremely complex to face the immense possibilities and related risks for 'intangibles' to be disseminated speedily and anonymously through the Internet in particular. In parallel, official services face great difficulties to properly carry out their controls and efficiently master constantly evolving technology, information networks, and communication means that are more and more difficult to monitor efficiently. Governments face difficulties to

[10]Aubin and Pang (2000).

implement streamlined and fully compliant export control systems that do not impair companies' competitiveness. This is probably one of the unsaid reasons why, some years ago, governmental export control authorities agreed without too many difficulties and even promoted, 'ex post' controls. Accordingly, today, industry is fully responsible for the full compliance of exports, and companies must manage the related risks. In practice, exporters have to guarantee the full traceability of their operations, from the procurement of foreign components to be integrated in sale products, up to the ultimate end use of the exported systems.

Such a heavy responsibility imposes the obligation for exporting companies to organise close management of the compliance to export control laws and regulations on their suppliers or partners. Integrators, in particular, must ensure that the entire business chain is immune from any risks that would jeopardise their international activities and/or reputation. In addition to the classical scrutiny of governmental agencies through the public procurement rules, the soundness of the compliance and the compliance organisation of the supplier, especially in export control laws and regulations have become decisive selection criteria for a huge number of companies. Companies need to be sure that they do not expose themselves to fines and criminal sanctions but, above all, that they have, daily, no risk of delayed shipments, leading possibly to face heavy contractual damages. Particular attention is more and more often paid to contractual provisions throughout the supply chain (which is in general long and complex in the international context), in order for contractors to be protected as much a possible *vis-à-vis* their suppliers as well as their clients.

In respect of foreign investment, for instance, to incorporate a subsidiary or to create a joint venture company with a local partner) in military or dual-use sectors, the buyer must clearly know and understand the constraints on the national laws and regulations in respect of goods and technologies exports and re-export control issues. Prior to any binding operation, the investing company has to understand the specific provisions and related business risks of the local laws limiting, as the case may be, foreign investments in sectors related to military or dual-use goods. In particular, when the purchased company has some military or dual-use activities, to determine the value of the company and the potential liabilities, the buyer carries out a 'due diligence' on the company to be purchased. The assessment of the value and possible risks of the targeted company are managed by the buying company. A usual practice is to check and assess the targeted company's military and/or dual-use licenses. This, in particular, ensures that the targeted company is authorised to deliver all contemplated controlled equipment to its customers in authorised countries and, accordingly, can benefit from the revenues flowing from the related sale contracts.

To add to that complexity of official laws and regulations, in recent years 'soft laws' have come into play. As a result, this new 'fashion' sometimes makes certain stakeholders go beyond the provisions of governmental laws and attempts to influence companies in making certain decisions (up to sale restrictions). In that respect, 'civil society', in particular NGOs, lead increasingly public actions through mass media, while traditional economic stakeholders such as regulatory bodies and ratings agencies or so-called 'ethical investment funds' make their own soft laws that are more and more over-compliant with the governmental legal demands. Therefore, increasingly, companies are obliged to develop general compliance and ethical programs. When implemented, new compliance rules first affect the most operational functions, that is, production, marketing, and sale of goods and services, and then the product supply chain follows up with the procurement and even mergers and acquisition activities and investment markets.

Due to the need to trace all military items once they are exported to ensure that they are not re-exported in infringement of any laws or regulations, the US and the UK governments, in particular, have developed an extensive notion of jurisdiction. Such an approach results from the idea that domestic jurisdiction applies wherever related domestic components should be exported. It conflicts with other countries' sovereignty and traditional rules of international public laws. Of course, this approach is only possible for countries of significant international importance from economical and/or political perspectives. This is why, fortunately, no other countries have adopted this attitude, which indeed is officially condemned by the EU.[11] Nevertheless, the US extraterritoriality must be underlined. Given the reach of US export control laws and regulations, and the weight of US technologies in today's world, it is very likely that there will be US content in many goods or services exported, and that the exporter will have to ensure compliance (as well as that of his suppliers or sub-contractors) with US laws and regulations. For companies, it is of essence to take that into account particularly, and it makes for strong awareness (information, training, education, and so forth) about the American control export requirements, both in the military (ITAR) and commercial (EAR) domains. This compliance with the US rules demands that industry takes particular care of supplies, storage, integration, and sales (specific management of end-uses and end-users) as the Americans refer to their own national (black) lists of products, countries, and persons. Of course, non-US companies can try to escape the US laws and regulations and refrain from buying any American product. However, such a strategy has never been very realistic, and this is all the more so that such companies should have assets or interests in the US.[12] The complexity, for a company wishing to comply with the relevant applicable export control laws and regulations, is obviously very important. Such an exporting company must take into account its domestic laws (i.e., the laws of the country from which exports are made) but also the laws of the supply chain (suppliers/sub-contractors, business partners, logistics, and so forth). Exporting companies must, in most cases, ensure up to 100% that the final exported product will be shipped to the country of final

[11]Cf.: Council Regulation (EC) No 2271/96 of 22 November 1996, protecting against the effects of the extra-territorial application of legislation adopted by a third country, and actions based thereon or resulting therefrom. http://eur-lex.europa.eu/LexUriServ/LexUriServ.do?uri=CELEX:31996R2271:EN:HTML.

[12]These questions have attracted wide media coverage at least in Europe and general Medias have dealt with this. See e.g., Laurent Zecchini, 'Le 'Code de conduite' de l'UE est censé servir de garde-fou aux exportations d'armements', Le Monde, 16 April 2005, p. 6.

destination and will be well received by the designated end-user. Moreover, sometimes the laws of the country of destination are to be considered; it could append for instance in the case of local import particularities. Lastly, in certain complex operations, additional specific laws and regulations from other jurisdictions need to be taken into account. This could be the case when experiments or tests need to be done on equipment in the development and/or manufacturing phases in countries that are different from the country of manufacturing, final assembly, or final destination. The addition of layers upon layers of legislation increases dramatically, of course, the cost of the compliance that could be, at the end, very high. One can note here that, at this particular point, (also linked to security of supply issue) was the subject of many debates within the European Community Member states during the preparation of the ICT Directive (EC 43/2009) set up for Intra-Community Transfers of 'defence related products.'

5.2 How an International Group Can Manage Its Business with Sanctions Countries: The Airbus Group Case

From its origin, Airbus Group has been in charge of military projects but, for many years, 80% of the company's products were civil passenger aircraft. Activities are essentially shared between five 'home countries': France, Germany, Spain, the UK, and the US. The company is oriented towards cutting-edge technologies and high value added products.

Airbus Group treats military and dual use exports in full compliance with the specific regulations and related controls of the different countries where it develops its business. Indeed, Airbus Group has customers and suppliers all over the world. In addition, this multinational activity is made even more complex by the native structure of the company tailored to work within a collaborative business model.

It is in this general context that Airbus Group is naturally looking very closely at all export compliance issues. The first mission of the Group's Export Control Compliance organisation is to support and give the best objective and consistent solutions, throughout its top executives, project managers, sales teams, and of course customers. Our banking partners are probably the most challenging to reach!... Indeed, within the company, we are able to convince everyone, since we all work towards the same goal. However, when we need to talk to governmental services or financial partners, we increasingly need to justify our decisions. This is why, as soon as 2005, following the particularly difficult sale of a purely civilian (A 321 model) passenger aircraft to the Iranian presidency, the Group decided to set up a very clear and practical policy, as well as useful guidelines to assess, recommend, and finally accept or not accept each and every contemplated business with 'sensitive countries.'

Regarding exports, we pay attention to the three pillars of sensitive product control: (1) the product functions and performances, (2) the end user, and (3) the end use. At Airbus Group, we use traditional tools. Before signing the sale contract, we set recommendations based on official published lists, independent studies, due diligences, and of course common sense—what Americans call 'red flags'; e.g.: customers who want to pay in cash, customers who do not ask for after sale support and maintenance conditions, and so forth... Before shipping products or delivering services or disclosing controlled information, we ask for official compliance agreements and/or certifications. We also often demand end-user and/or end-use commitments and international importation certificates; we may add contractual re-export clauses; we take particular care of exchanges of 'Controlled Unclassified Information' (CUI); finally, we do not hesitate to consult (formally or not…) and ask for the assistance of our respective national official services. Indeed we know that we can rely on national official services, we consider as a duty to be very fair and transparent, giving and justifying our respective authorities the reasons why we want to go ahead and offer them guarantees to ensure a full compliance in our operations.

The export control challenge is the following: how can we reduce the risks lying within the products and/or destination sensitivity and mitigate them? As soon as one explains people managing sales why it is forbidden to sell sophisticated products to particular customers, they can accept not to do it, considering the business sake and the company's reputation. Hence, instead of always acting like firemen, we naturally reduce the risks well beforehand by sensitisation, training, and support. A particularly complex domain is R&D. It is not, today, too much difficult to tag and trace "tangible goods", moreover it is increasingly easy to achieve it very well with the efficient support of IT systems. However at the same time, such IT tool could certainly be the worst enemy of export control compliance. People, traditionally at all times, were used to carry information and share, "physically", even their most sensitive knowledge with their foreign counterparts in meetings and seminars. Today, in an international company, engineers and technicians need permanent links to exchange on their projects with their counterparts worldwide. Collaboration, teamwork, multi-parallel experiments, and so forth make the best of our engineering and creativity power! Computers, networks, workflows, and electronics for more powerful communications, mean having no frontiers, and make it nearly impossible to efficiently control such intangible transfers.

From an organisational perspective, the export control function of the Airbus Group, (a 134,000-employee company), is structured around 130 full time specialists. We are not able to fully control by ourselves all the international business and exchanges. Accordingly, we have no other choice than to be efficient and aware, to educate and train our colleagues, on each and every service of the Group, about export risks and export control laws and regulations commitments. The main message is indeed quite simple: *Think export control and ask, your export compliance officer.*

To address the export control compliance risk at the earliest possible stage of the process, we set up, since 2005, the so-called 'CEO's Sanctioned Countries Procedure'. At the beginning, we tried to list the 'sensitive' countries from a business point of view (i.e. the ones for which we had trouble obtaining licences from our export control authorities (e.g.: Taiwan). We chose, very early on, not to tackle the most 'sensitive' countries but rather the 'officially sanctioned' ones. The rational of that decision is quite easy to understand, as one can find its origin in the very nature of industrial companies. On the one hand, Industry must comply with national and international laws and regulations made to ensure the security of nations, that governments set up and enforce in the framework of their respective foreign policy. On the other hand, the companies' have to produce, sell, and possibly export but, for sure, not to interfere in governmental foreign policy. Moreover, for international or transnational groups such as Airbus, it is extremely difficult to find a general agreement between five countries that have five different foreign policies, and it is properly impossible to even define any internal 'soft law,' because following all political restrictions of each 'home country' should lead to dramatically impair the business and even totally block it. Accordingly, we figured out that for some of our customers, being rated 'sensitive' and ending up next to countries like North Korea, Sudan, or Syria could be very problematic businesswise, and moreover should possibly be detrimental for side diplomatic efforts. Accordingly, to prevent debates we decided to publish a list strictly limited to officially sanctioned countries only. Finally, and above all, we totally comply with the fundamental Group's position, which is to, strictly and only, comply with governmental demands, not to make any own foreign policy. As an industrial company, we consider clearly that it is not our responsibility to self-decide whether a country is, or not, politically correct or what could be its diplomatic relations with the Group's home countries. Whereas when we speak of sanctioned countries there is no doubt left: we take into account UN and EU sanctions lists and, when necessary, those of our home countries. For each customer country, we calculate a score by simple addition of sanctions made by international institutions and our home countries governments.

Practically, as of the Sanctioned Country Process, the compliance system relies on two pillars. The first one is constituted of a quarterly updated list of sanctioned countries. This list is distributed to all our project managers to make them unambiguously aware to which countries it will be difficult to eventually export. To compile the 'Sanctioned Country List', we consult only the official Internet sites. We take much care to remain strictly factual. Based on this list, we established the following single commitment for exporters: 'you must report the Group CEO, as soon as you contemplate business with one listed country'. The most difficult export compliance assessments concern countries that are not officially sanctioned; for these countries, we have elaborated on a 'sensitivity indicator.' This is the second pillar of the Sanctioned Country Process. It takes into account economics, human rights, and social development factors that can jeopardise the image of the Group *vis-à-vis* media and shareholders. Those are basic and standard export control principles that all governments use to rely on to grant export licenses. A prior assessment of these criteria allows Airbus Group to secure business by anticipating difficulties to eventually get the governmental shipment authorisation. More precisely, we consider two socio-economic indicators (the economic stability of the customer's country and its social development), and two ethical indicators (corruption level and human rights compliance).

Thanks to the 'SCP', Airbus assesses and documents with a sound, rational, and consistent methodology all its most sensitive business cases. Accordingly the Group is in the position, to face in good conditions any possible audit, inquiry or charge and advocate for export decisions made by its divisions, affiliates, and subsidiaries.

5.3 Conclusion

Export control matters are very complex. This complexity increases more and more and, due to governments "ex-post control" policy, companies are totally responsible for full compliance in this area of law. Mitigating that risk requires companies to appoint experts in order to implement, manage, and develop sound internal export compliance organisation. Accordingly, industry experts and academics should address as soon as possible this new challenge together and organise the best answer to each government's international expectations by selecting and educating their future national elites of export control.

References

Aubin, Yann, and Xiaoman Pang. 2000. Should an investment be ethical and can it be so? *International Business Law Review* 7: 857–878.

Jean-Claude Martinez. 1983. Le droit international et le commerce des armes. In Société française pour le droit international, 'Le droit international et les. The same was true in the Nations Society Pact [which was the organization prevailing prior to the United Nations], edited by A. Pedone, p. 115.

Chapter 6
Export Control Constraints from a Contractual Point of View

Marc Borello

Abstract This article describes how international contracts deal with export control constraints. The burden and risks of non issuance or cancellation of export licences may be on the side of one party only (buyer or seller) or be shared, up to a certain extent, between the parties. The contract may also grant to the parties some time to find alternative solutions, if this can work.

Large international contracts for the supply of equipment or systems using high-value technologies are always subject to export control contingencies. Most of the time, complex equipment or systems incorporate parts originating from more than one country. This has two consequences in terms of export control constraints. First, it implies that the end product (e.g., the whole system) is subject to export control rules from its country of origin where it is designed, developed, and assembled, and whence it is exported. Secondly, components and parts that are procured may also be subject to export control contingencies of the countries whence they are procured. These parts or components from other countries may also affect the exportability of the whole equipment or system.

As a result, the export of complex equipment or systems very frequently needs more than one export license: one license (relating to the final equipment or system) from the country to which the end product will be exported, and, as the case may be, a license or licenses (in relation only to parts or components) from the country or countries whence the parts or components are procured. This implies that non-issuance of the export license for a single component originating from another country will prevent the export of the whole system that incorporates that component—even if an export license is granted by the country exporting the end product.

Marc Borello has a Ph.D. in law from the Sorbonne University, Paris (1983), and has been general counsel in various defense and aerospace companies.

M. Borello (✉)
Paris, France
e-mail: f6drw@orange.fr

D. Tamada and P. Achilleas (eds.), *Theory and Practice of Export Control*,
Kobe University Social Science Research Series,
DOI 10.1007/978-981-10-5960-5_6

The contract may provide different solutions to a nonissuance, subsequent modification, or cancellation of an export license. The fact that these export licenses come from the country where the system or equipment will be exported or from a country where some parts or components are manufactured and incorporated into the end product does not change the situation and contract solutions typically address both issues the same way.

Issues in relation to export licenses make take different shapes. Here are some examples:

- Embargo. An embargo may take its origin from a decision made by the General Assembly of the United Nations and subsequently incorporated by each country into its legal system (embargoes relating to North Korea or Iran, for example) or by the European Union (EU) if issued as an EU Regulation directly applicable to each EU member state (for instance, Russia following the Ukraine crisis). An embargo may also be decreed unilaterally by a country, like the United States embargoes toward Vietnam and Cuba. It is important to note that an embargo taking its origin from a decision of the United Nations may be implemented differently, being more or less stringent, in each country's legal system. An embargo may be total, with a general prohibition on any export to, or import from, the target country; this was the case with the United States' embargo on Cuba. Alternatively, it can be specific, prohibiting only some types of products or services, or prohibiting commercial or financial relations with a list of persons or companies; an example is the European Union's embargo on Russia. An embargo may prohibit any future contract after a specific date, thus may allow exports under contracts already in force. The embargo may prohibit both, i.e., it may suspend exports under contracts already signed and prohibit any future contracts.
- No export license granted. The refusal by a government to grant an export license may arise in different circumstances. Political circumstances may have changed in a matter of months, and thus a license that would have been easy to obtain could become an issue. If the license is needed before contract signature, the contract usually provides that there is no coming into force if the license is not granted. If the license is needed after the contract comes into force but before export of the item, the parties will have to solve the issue, as we will see later on.
- Modification or cancellation of an existing export license. The practical consequences in this situation are not very different from the previous case. The modification may have retroactive effect or may be applicable only from the date it is made known to the public.
- Wrong classification by a component manufacturer. This situation arises in countries where the classification of the components is left to the exporter according to guidelines issued by the administration (like the United States). The manufacturer initially classifies the component in the wrong category, e.g., as a "freely exportable" component. Afterward, the manufacturer changes the classification of the same component into a "not freely exportable" category,

therefore subject to export constraints. Meanwhile the contract for sale of the equipment or system may be already in force with the end user, and sometimes the component may be already assembled in the equipment or system. This change of classification may result from an administrative instruction received from the component manufacturer after, for example, an audit performed by its administration.

Contract provisions dealing with these issues provide very different solutions, depending on the type of product, the context, and the bargaining power of each party. First, the contract may provide that export control issues are solely the burden of the seller and any problem with an export license will be a seller's default. Secondly, the contract may provide the exact opposite: that export licenses shall be obtained by the buyer, and the seller shall have no liability in relation to these licenses. Thirdly, the contract may be more balanced between the parties, providing that the seller is excused for some time from performance of the contract due to an export control issue and, after a certain period of time, the contract will be terminated at seller's cost, buyer's cost, or cost shared between the parties. Fourthly, the contract may provide that termination is not the solution and the parties will share the cost for the use of alternatives to the component or product that cannot be exported due to export constraints. Of course, this fourth solution is impossible in the case of an embargo.

Contract solutions to these issues may be divided into three broad categories:

- *The first category* is to leave export control issues as an exclusive burden of one of the parties and a cause for termination of the contract due to default. This will be discussed in Part One, "Export control issues as the exclusive burden of the buyer or the seller."
- *The second category* is to consider an export control issue as excusable delay or a case of force majeure, allowing the seller to postpone the delivery of the procured item in order to find a solution, and leading ultimately to termination of the contract if this is found to be impossible. This will be discussed in Part Two, "Export control issues considered as a case of force majeure with termination of the contract if no solution is found."
- *The third category* is similar: an export control issues is considered excusable delay or a case of force majeure, and the seller is allowed to postpone delivery to find a solution. The difference from the second category is that a procedure is put in place describing the possible solution and sharing the cost between the parties. As we will see, this may or may not lead ultimately to termination of the contract. This will be discussed in Part Three, "Export control issues considered as a case of force majeure, with alternative solutions proposed."

6.1 Part One: Export Control Issues as the Exclusive Burden of the Buyer or the Seller

Export control issues not considered a force majeure event. Although it sounds unreasonable for a party to accept such an extreme solution, a party may sometimes accept the risk in a context where it has absolutely no control and cannot interfere in any manner in the grant of a license that a government will issue in its absolute discretion. For example, such risk may be accepted without any problem where the goods are already existing and are in the hands of the seller, and export licenses are already granted. The contract can be signed and the goods can be delivered to the buyer in a few days without any risk for the seller. In this context, as well as in any other circumstances where risks are very limited, the seller can accept this kind of contract solution.

Example of clause. Here is an example of a clause where exportability of the purchased items is the seller's firm commitment and nondelivery of such items due to export control issues shall be a case of termination for default:

> If any license or consent of any government or other authority shall be required for the acquisition, carriage, storage, or use of the procured goods by Buyer, Seller shall obtain the same at its own expense and, if necessary, produce evidence of the same to Buyer on demand. Seller hereby declares that all necessary export licenses required to perform this contract have been granted or shall be granted, if not issued yet, for the timely delivery of the procured goods. Nonissuance, modification, or withdrawal of any required export license shall be considered a default of Seller entitling Buyer to terminate this contract at Seller's cost according to Article …, "Termination of the Contract for Default."

Consequences: payment of liquidated damages for delay and termination for default. The consequences of this solution are extreme: the export control issue is considered an event of default, and this will have two consequences for the seller. The first consequence will be the payment of liquidated damages for late delivery if the contract contains such a clause. The second consequence will be termination for default. After some days or weeks to cure the default, if the goods still cannot be exported, the buyer may terminate the contract for seller's default. The termination will be usually ab initio, which means that (i) all payments received by the seller before termination will be repaid to the buyer, and (ii) the seller will keep the property (or the work in progress if the goods were under construction at the time of termination). Unless the contract provides some limit or exclusion of liability, the buyer shall be entitled to claim damages against the seller for nonperformance of the contract and to obtain from the seller the difference of price if the buyer has to buy similar goods from a third party at a higher price.

Obviously, the wording may be turned around to provide the same solution but put the burden and costs on the buyer instead. The buyer may accept such a solution if he deems that the risk is nonexistent or very low. In this case, obviously, there will be no liquidated damages for late delivery of damages or for procuring the goods from a third party.

6.2 Part Two: Export Control Issues Considered a Case of Force Majeure, with Termination of the Contract if no Solution Is Found

Since the parties have no control over government decisions banning or restricting the export of goods or services to some countries, most often they will consider export control issues as a form of force majeure, and the contract will provide solutions along these lines.

Export control issues considered a force majeure event. In this Part Two, export control bans are considered force majeure or excusable delay, granting the seller additional time to find a solution. At the end of the additional time period, if the contract is still impacted by the export control prohibition, it will be terminated. Financial consequences of any such termination, as we will see, will be the sole burden of the seller or the buyer, or may be shared between buyer and seller.

From a contract standpoint, export control matters can be addressed without any specific clause, e.g., mixed with other provisions dealing with force majeure, or can be the subject matter of contract provisions dedicated to export control.

Examples of clauses. Here is an example of clause merging export control issues into general provisions relating to force majeure:

> Seller shall not be in default for failure in the performance of this contract if such failure constitutes a case of force majeure. Force majeure, as used herein, shall mean any abnormal impediment or occurrence that prevents the fulfillment of this contract and which Seller had no reason to take into account when entering into this contract and which could not be averted or prevented without unreasonable expense or loss of time. Such case may result, for instance, from war, mutiny, internal unrest, expropriation or confiscation for public needs, any act of government, embargo, nonissuance, modification or cancellation of export license, acts of God, discontinuation of public transportation or supply or energy, conflicts or strikes of any kind, fire, or some other event(s) beyond the control of Seller. If the force majeure event does not cease after a period of ….. days, Buyer shall be entitled to terminate this contract according to Article ….

Here is an example of a dedicated clause dealing specifically with export control issues:

> This contract is subject to all applicable laws and regulations relating to the export of the system and to all applicable laws and regulations of the country or countries to which it will be exported, which are countries A, B, and C, with the exclusion of any other country. Without limiting the scope of this clause, Contractor shall use its reasonable best efforts to obtain all approvals and licenses required by the laws and regulations of the country or countries to which the system will be exported or declared to be exported under this contract. Purchaser shall use its reasonable best efforts to obtain all government approvals and licenses to export the system to these countries: A, B, and C.
>
> If a government refuses to grant a required approval or license to export the system, or revokes or suspends an approval or license subsequent to its grant, or grants a license or approval subject to conditions, that shall be considered an event of force majeure. In that event, (i) this contract shall nevertheless remain in full force and effect and (ii) the delivery schedule shall be adjusted on a day-for-day basis for each day that Contractor is impacted by such action or inaction of such government. Such government action or inaction shall

not modify in any way the rights and obligations of the parties under this contract except to relieve Contractor of any obligations that cannot be performed without such an approval or license.

The parties confirm that their performance of, and obligations under, this contract are in all matters subject to the provisions of this Article.

Purchaser hereby acknowledges that licenses granted in relation to the system are limited to countries A, B, and C and that re-export by Purchaser to any country other than these three countries shall need additional licenses that will have to be sought by Purchaser directly from the concerned authorities. Contractor does not grant Purchaser any warranty whatsoever in relation to the possible issuance or nonissuance of licenses from any country other than A, B, and C.

Should the force majeure event not have ceased after a period of …. days, Purchaser shall be entitled to terminate this contract according to Article ….

Despite their different wording and a much more precise mechanism in the second clause, the solutions granted are similar: the seller will be excused in relation to issues relating to export control and, after some specified time, the contract will be terminated for force majeure.

Consequences: termination for force majeure. A force majeure or excusable delay event due to an export control issue will postpone the delivery date of the goods for a specified time. The duration of such period is left to the parties and will be usually from 15 to 180 days, depending on the parties' assessment of the risk at the contract signing. An embargo, however, will not cease in 15 or even 180 days, and in such case an extended period of time to find an alternative solution will not serve any purpose. Sometimes a solution can be found where the export control issue is a simple one, manageable by the seller.

In case of embargo, or if no solution can be found, the buyer can opt to terminate the contract. Consequences of a termination for force majeure are usually more balanced than for a termination for default, but there can be a combination of different elements, less or more favorable for a party. Here are some examples:

- *Termination less favorable for the seller and more favorable for the buyer*: All payments made before delivery are repaid to the buyer, and the seller remains the owner of all works in progress.
- *Termination more favorable for the seller and less favorable for the buyer*: The seller will be repaid all costs sustained due to the termination, but not lost profits. All works in progress will remain the property of the seller, who shall use his best endeavors to reuse them in a contract with a third party. If he succeeds, his proceeds from such third party shall be rendered to the buyer.
- *In both cases*: The buyer cannot claim any damages against the seller due to such termination.

6.3 Part Three: Export Control Issues Considered a Case of Force Majeure, with Alternative Solutions Proposed

In this Part Three, similar to Part Two, export control issues are considered excusable delay or force majeure, and the seller is allowed to postpone delivery and seek a solution. The difference is that a precise procedure is put in place in the contract, describing the possible solution and how costs are shared between the parties. As we will see, this may or may not lead ultimately to termination of the contract if the specified solution is found impossible.

Export control issues considered a force majeure event, with specific solution. The solution sought by the parties will be to replace the problematic component(s) with new components that do not have problems in terms of export control. Most of the time, this will imply significant modifications to the equipment or to the system using the problematic component(s). At contract level, the first step will be to grant time to the parties to elaborate a workable solution. The second step will be to implement the solution through the signing of a contract change

This approach will be used when the parties do not want export control issues to force an immediate solution of contract termination. This will depend, of course, on the type of equipment or system involved, the quantity sold, and the time frame of the delivery(ies).

Example of clause.

Governmental Authorizations:

As of the effective date of contract, Seller warrants and represents that the deliverable items have been designed and the suppliers and subcontractors selected, such that the deliverable items can be exported to Buyer's country in accordance with this contract.

Seller shall at its own expense submit in due time all proper and correct applications to obtain and maintain in force and effect all governmental authorizations and licenses required for the performance of its obligations and for timely delivery of the deliverable items to their contract point of delivery. These governmental authorizations and licenses shall cover the export from the country of manufacture of the deliverable Items and from the country of origin of any parts thereof and of any technical data and information that will be required in the performance of the contract.

Buyer shall, at its own expense, obtain and maintain in force and effect all governmental authorizations required for Buyer's performance of its obligations under this contract.

Each party undertakes to provide the other party with all reasonable support (including provision of data and information or signature of documents) as may be requested by the other party and which may be necessary to obtain or maintain governmental authorizations.

Recovery Plan Following an Export Control Issue:

Notwithstanding any other provisions to the contrary, from the period beginning at the effective date of this contract and ending upon arrival of the deliverable items at their contract point of delivery, if any event not attributable to Seller results in the prevention of delivery of the deliverable items at their contract point of delivery, Seller shall promptly inform Buyer in writing. Following such notice, the parties shall agree upon reasonable appropriate alternative solutions, if any, to remedy the delay, implemented in respect of the deliverable items (the "Recovery Plan") within thirty (30) days from the date of Buyer's receipt of Seller's notice, or any other period of time agreed upon by the parties. The Recovery Plan shall be implemented at Seller's cost. If the mutually agreed Recovery Plan results in an extension of time of the delivery date and/or adjustment of any other provision of this contract (except price), Seller shall be granted an extension of time and this contract shall be amended accordingly.

Failure to Agree on Recovery Plan:

Should the parties fail to agree upon the Recovery Plan within the thirty (30) day period or any other period agreed upon by the parties, or if the Recovery Plan will result in an extension of time of the delivery date by more than … days, or if the parties are unable to agree upon the amendment to be made to the contract within thirty (30) days from Seller's notice to claim an extension of time and/or modification of any other affected contract provision, Buyer will have the right to terminate this contract according to Article ….

Consequences. The implications of these contract provisions can be summarized in five points:

- *First point*: At the contract's effective date, the equipment or system sold, as designed and manufactured, can be exported to the buyer's country without any restriction. This implies that this equipment or system has been carefully developed, designed, and manufactured to address any export control constraints. Industrially speaking, this implies a long process before contract signature in which export control constraints are carefully taken into consideration in designing the product, including coordination with subcontractors and low-tier suppliers before offering it for sale. This exercise has its limits and sometimes proves impossibly difficult.
- *Second point*: The seller commits that he will forthwith inform the buyer of any export control restriction that could appear after contract signing, as soon as any such restriction is known to him.
- *Third point*: The seller commits to proposing an alternative solution that does not use the problematic components or equipment, describing the impact in terms of delivery time (the Recovery Plan). This is probably the most important provision. This implies that the seller will undertake, if necessary, to redesign some part of the equipment since the chosen alternative component may have different technical characteristics from the previous one. Such modification may take many months. It is important to note that the clause does not mention the cost impact of the modification. As it is worded, the seller will bear the cost. Obviously the parties could reword the clause to provide a different agreed-upon solution, e.g., the buyer pays, or the cost is shared between the parties.
- *Fourth point*: The buyer commits to examine carefully the seller's proposal for an alternative solution and respond within a precise time frame. Obviously the seller must have proved his intention to go ahead with an alternative solution, provided that this solution does not impact too much the main purpose of the contract. The contract may identify some conditions for the buyer to accept the alternative solution; for instance, it could specify that the new delivery date cannot exceed a certain period compared to the initial date.
- *Fifth point*: The contract will typically identify a time frame for the new delivery under the alternative solution. If the solution is found workable, a contract

change will implement the solution. If no agreement is reached between the parties on the Recovery Plan (because the new delivery date exceeds the limits stated in the contract, for instance), the buyer shall have the right to terminate the contract for force majeure. The consequences for such termination are the ones mentioned at the end of Part Two.

6.4 Conclusion

Two points need to be mentioned in conclusion. The first is the importance of governing laws. As in any contract, the choice of governing laws will be crucial to define each party's rights and obligations and to interpret the contract in case of unclear contract provisions.

The second point is the importance of insurance. Up to a certain level, it is possible for the seller to insure some of the risks coming from an export control issue, whether with a public or private insurance company. Rates will vary depending on the type of product, the time for performing the contract, and the countries involved. The guarantees granted by insurance will usually provide a deductible and a maximum guaranteed limit. If the contract needs more than one export license, the insurance will usually become effective provided that at least the first license is granted at the very beginning of the contract performance. This has a cost, of course, but insurance may be a good solution to accept risks that without insurance would be totally unreasonable for the seller to bear.

Chapter 7
Effects and "Side Effects" of the Implementation of Trade Restrictions for European Economic Operators in the Field of Aerospace

Rosa Rosanelli

Abstract This article focuses on the challenges for Industries when implementing US export control regulations, applicable extra-territorially to hardware and technology originated in the United States. Interaction of US regulations with local export control restrictions and translation into practice of these multiple requirements may lead to contradictory obligations for non-US companies, and face compliance officers with the dilemma of nevertheless making these multiple requirements coexist in the Company's internal compliance program. This article advocates for forms of harmonization that go in the sense of international commitments on non-proliferation while facilitating compliance and a level-playing field for companies dealing with strategic goods.

Keywords ITAR · Extra-territoriality · Industry · Export control

7.1 Introduction

In the debate on "Theory and Practice of Export Control", this paper is aimed at highlighting the potential adverse consequences of trade restrictions for European businesses operating in the field of aerospace and defense. Whenever confronted with United States-origin items or technical information, contractors dealing with items classified as dual use or military operate in a "multi-layered" compliance scenario. As several sets of rules are enforced nationally as well as extra-territorially, significant investments are required to achieve a "mistake-proof" internal compliance program. At the same time, the implementation of trade restrictions may expose

R. Rosanelli (✉)
Belgium Engine Center, Herstal, Belgium
e-mail: rosa.rosanelli@bec.eu.com

R. Rosanelli
AIM Norway Group, Kjeller, Norway

D. Tamada and P. Achilleas (eds.), *Theory and Practice of Export Control*,
Kobe University Social Science Research Series,
DOI 10.1007/978-981-10-5960-5_7

the company to adverse effects such as potential conflicts of regulations, distortions of competition and un-level playing field between big businesses and SMEs.

7.2 Theory of Export Control: The Legal Basis of Trade Restrictions on Strategic Goods and Their Effect on European Business

Since the beginning of the 1950s, international trade agreements have always tended to limit unilateral restrictions on international trade. However, in order to allow national specific controls for goods and services related to weapons, dual-use items (but also cultural goods, for instance) a general exception and a security exception have been introduced in the GATT,[1] allowing Contracting States to adopt specific national restrictive measures.

Art. XXI, "Security exceptions", allows Contracting Parties to unilaterally derogate to GATT principles in a series of cases, notably whenever their application would hamper the implementation of international commitments undertaken under the UN Charter for the maintenance of international peace and security. An exception may also be invoked by a State party whenever "*necessary for the protection of its essential security interests*" including "*the traffic in arms, ammunition and implements of war*" and "*traffic in other goods and materials as is carried on directly or indirectly for the purpose of supplying a military establishment*".[2]

As the GATT does not define terms such as "*necessary*", "*essential security interests*", or even "*arms*" and "*implements of war*", exceptions may de facto apply to a very extensive list of items and possible scenarios. This appeared evident in 1949, when the United States claimed to be entitled under Art XXI to restrict shipments for "security reasons" in response to Czechoslovakia's protest after theEenactment of an embargo on a list of more than 200 items, even if certain export license denials "involved goods only remotely related to supplying military establishments".[3]

---

[1]Originally signed in 1947, the General Agreement on Tariffs and Trade ("GATT") is a multi-lateral agreement that regulates trade between 153 countries with the objective of "*substantial reduction of tariffs and other trade barriers and the elimination of preferences, on a reciprocal and mutually advantageous basis.*", https://www.wto.org/english/docs_e/legal_e/gatt47_01_e.htm.

[2]Q. Michel, S. Paile, M. Tsukanova, A. Viski, "Controlling the Trade of Dual-Use Goods: A Handbook", Non Proliferation and Security, Peter Lang, p. 27.

[3]US Department of State, Office of the Historian, "Foreign Relations of the United States 1949", Volume I, National Security Affairs, Foreign Economic Policy [Document 242] 560.AL/3–2249: Circular telegram https://history.state.gov/historicaldocuments/frus1949v01/d242; see also: P. Lindsay, "The Ambiguity of GATT Article XXI: Subtle Success or Rampant Failure?", 2003 p. 1293. Available: http://scholarship.law.duke.edu/cgi/viewcontent.cgi?article=1192&context=dlj and Q. Michel, S. Paile, M. Tsukanova, A. Viski, *cit.*, p. 31.

In 1950, the COCOM (Coordinating Committee for Multilateral Export Controls) was established as informal multilateral organization with the objective to coordinate the national controls applied by the United States and its allies over the export of strategic materials and technology to the other side of the "iron curtain". Trade restrictions have been adopted since then, with important implications for international trade in strategic goods.

Since the UN Security Council Resolution 1540, adopted in 2004 under Chapter VII and thus legally binding, all States have the obligation to adopt and enforce a minimum standard of domestic controls, including physical protection and trade control regimes. The international export control "regimes" are nevertheless generally structured in the form of "fora", adopting guidelines that are not prescriptive in nature and therefore not directly applicable.

While the Arms Trade Treaty may in the future pave the way to more stringent provisions and to a more structured harmonization in the domain of military-classified items, as of today international coordination and exchange of communications still takes place in *fora* of discussion such as the Wassenaar Arrangement, the most influential in promoting transparency, thanks to the publication of best practices and a key role played in the establishment of harmonized control lists.

Their informal nature and the non-legally binding character of their guidelines inevitably entail further transposition procedures, with a risk that implementation is either unharmonized or delayed from one country to another.[4] Eventually implementation will be done with in mind country-specific concerns and strategic interests, and with nuances in their interpretation and in the incorporation in national provisions.

7.3 Export Controls in Practice: A "Multi-layered" Compliance Scenario

In addition to laws and regulations of the country in which they are established, European businesses, notably when operating in sectors that are typically linked to an actual or potential military application, need to encompass a multitude of regulations in their compliance schemes.

A company established in the European Union will need to take into account applicable European Regulations and embargoes adopted by the UN Security Council, but also the law of the respective countries of suppliers and subcontractors and eventually the laws of the country of the customer. In general, export controls can play a key role in supply chain coordination, and can influence the company's ability to respect contractual obligations.

---

[4]For instance, the 2011 Wassenaar changes took two years to be implemented in Europe, resulting in discrepancies amongst lists of controls.

In addition to these sets of rules, whenever confronted with United States-origin items or technical information, US unilateral export control regulations also need to be taken into account, as a result of their "extra-territorial" enforcement on the territory of other countries. In this context, American export controls represent an additional burden for European companies.[5]

As a result of theories of extended jurisdiction, the United States attributes nationality to items originated in the country: whenever these items are listed in specific "control lists", regulations protecting US technology dissemination will apply on the items, wherever located.

While no specific rules of international law govern the "nationality" of goods other than aircrafts or ships, the legal concept of "nationality" was in itself developed almost exclusively for persons, in terms of diplomatic or consular protection, as the status or relationship that gives a nation the right to protect a person from other nations.[6] Several courts thus rejected US jurisdictional claim and refused to recognise the right to prohibit the export of goods situated on the territory of another country.[7]

International law attributes to sovereign States the exclusive ability to discipline behavior on its territory. However, based on the 'effects doctrine' the United States argue that its national jurisdiction may apply "extra-territorially",[8] since events happening elsewhere in the world, but which are related to US technology and can have an impact on US territory, are subject to US laws.[9]

It has been argued that the attribution to the sovereign State of the monopoly of organized armed force is -in itself- in contrast with the exercise of a normative competence on the territory of another country.[10] In other terms, a State cannot resort to coerce "*legal implementation measures such as penalties, fines, seizures,*

[5]R. Rosanelli, "US Export Control Regulations Explained to the European Exporter: A Handbook", University of Liège, January 2014. Available: http://local.droit.ulg.ac.be/jcms/service/index.php?serv=49&cat=3.

[6]D. Ehlers, "European Fundamental Rights and Freedoms", Berlin: De Gruyter Recht. pp. 547–548.

[7]In the American President Lines case, the Supreme Court of Hong Kong found that once discharged, the *lex situs* should apply to commodities present on the territory of Hong Kong and that any attempt to exercise US jurisdiction would be "an incursion into the sovereign rights" of the State. *American President Lines v. China Mutual Trading Company*, 1952 A.M.C. 1510, 1526 (Hong Kong Supreme Court). See also Moens v. Ahlers North German Lloyd, 30 R.W. 360 (Tribunal of Commerce, Antwerp 1966).

[8]In this paper, the terms "extra-territorial" and "extra-territoriality" typically refer to "*the application of a norm or a decision by the State from which they are issued, which is not achieved totally on the territory of the latter*", and in particular to the extra-territorial application *stricto* sensu, where the State claims the ability to produce legal effects outside of its territory, as described in: B Stern, "Quelques Observations sur les Règles Internationales Relatives à l'Application Extra-territoriale du Droit", Annuaire français de droit international, 1986, vol. 32, n. 1, p. 9.

[9]Q. Genard, "European Union responses to Extraterritorial Claims by the United States: Lessons From Trade Control Cases", *Non-Proliferation Papers*, No. 36 January 2014, p. 3.

[10]B. Stern, *cit.*, p. 22.

investigations or demands for information to give extraterritorial effect to its rules".[11]

As clarified by the Permanent Court of International Justice in the *Lotus* case, States may issue legislation that governs situations susceptible to take place abroad, in the absence of a contrary rule. Nevertheless, it is commonly accepted that this does not entitle them to enforce their laws outside their territory, "*except by virtue of a permissive rule derived from international custom or from a convention*."[12] Monetary judgments, for instance, could only be enforced by seizing located assets on the national territory of the enforcing State, or alternatively by international cooperation with the State where the defendant's assets are located.[13]

However, US courts have, during the past years, construed a theory of jurisdictial jurisdiction based on "minimum contacts", whereby their jurisdiction may be asserted based on the mere presence of a subsidiary of a foreign corporation in the United States or a transient presence on the US territory.[14] Recent cases of enforcement on financial institutions, such as BNP Paribas have shown how this jurisdiction may be "tagged" even if at one given moment in time economic transactions are transformed in US dollars.[15]

As highlighted in the *Lotus* case, there is a considerable difference between the right of a State to prescribe a behavior that has extra-territorial effects and the direct enforcement on the territory of another State, which de facto limits the sovereign authority of the latter. In other words, extra-territoriality would not in itself be in violation of international law principles, and its enforcement may be compatible with those principles if carried out "territorially": i.e. by suing the alledged violator in the territory of the State that enacted the territorial norm, threatening seizure of assets on its territory, banning his/her access to its territory or the possibility to register with a governmental agency and apply for export licenses.[16]

---

[11]C. Ryngaert, "Jurisdiction in International Law: United States and European Perspectives", Unpublished Ph.D. dissertation, Katholieke Universiteit Leuven, 2007. Available: https://lirias.kuleuven.be/bitstream/1979/911/2/doctoraat.pdf, p. 35.

[12]In the *Lotus* Case, the Court made an important distinction between the ability of a State to prescribe its rules—in the absence of a contrary rule—and enforcement of a State's laws on the territory of another State: "*[T]he first and foremost restriction imposed by international law upon a State is that—failing the existence of a permissive rule to the contrary—it may not exercise its power in any form in the territory of another State. In this sense jurisdiction is certainly territorial; it cannot be exercised by a State outside its territory except by virtue of a permissive rule derived from international custom or from a convention.*" Permanent Court of International Justice, *S.S. Lotus*, P.C.I.J. Reports, Series A, No. 10, pp. 18–19 (1927).

[13]C. Ryngaert, *cit.*, p. 23.

[14]C. Ryngaert, *cit.*, p. 23.

[15]US Department of Justice, "BNP Paribas Sentenced for Conspiring to Violate the International Emergency Economic Powers Act and the Trading with the Enemy Act", May 1, 2015 https://www.justice.gov/opa/pr/bnp-paribas-sentenced-conspiring-violate-international-emergency-economic-powers-act-and.

[16]C. Ryngaert, *cit.*, p. 36.

It has also been argued that a key element to determine legality of extra-territorial jurisdiction would be whether or not this behavior infringes upon the rights of other sovereign States, and ultimately be linked to the existence of a *permissive jurisdictional principle* under international law, and thus a "legitimate interest" an activity, that would nevertheless be accepted in the common practice.[17]

When we turn from theory to practice, it is nevertheless evident that aside from the legal analysis, extra-territorial enforcement is a "function of relative power".[18] When extra-territorial regulations are enforced by an economically powerful country, and foreign availability of the items or technology is limited, compliance with these requirement becomes ineluctable and essential for a company to be able to continue operating on the market and ultimately ensure its durability and the continuity of its business.

7.4 Extra-territoriality of Export Controls in the European Union

International trade has traditionally been a key element of cohesion in the history and identity of the European Union. In this sense, it has been argued that the size of its single market and its long experience in negotiating international trade agreements have made the EU a "trade power".[19]

Yet, when it comes to dual-use or military items, all European companies dealing with US-origin controlled technology and hardware strive to ensure full compliance with US regulations. A growing number of enforcement cases over entities located abroad, and notably on the territory of the European Union, has led to make compliance with US export control requirements an utmost priority when establishing an internal compliance program.

In fact, the legality of the extra-territorial enforcement of US regulations has been object of debate in the European Union.

Already in the 1980s, the Legal Service of the European Commission expressed concern vis-à-vis the extraterritorial impact of economic restrictions, announced by the Reagan administration in reactions to the state of emergency and suspension of some civil liberties in Poland.

---

[17]R.Y. Jennings, "Extraterritorial Jurisdiction in the United States Antitrust Laws", 33 Brit. Y.B. of International Law, 146, 1957 ("*It is reasonable to say ... that international law will permit a State to exercise extraterritorial jurisdiction provided that State's legitimate interests (legitimate that is to say be tests accepted in the common practice of States) are involved …*").

[18]"*Powerful States will be able to impose their legislation on weaker States, while weaker States will almost never be able to impose their legislation on more powerful States.*" C. Ryngaert, *cit.*, p. 45.

[19]S. Meunier, K. Nicolaïdis, 'The European Union as a conflicted trade power', *Journal of European Public Policy*, vol. 13, n. 6, Sep. 2006, p. 917.

The measures concerned licensing requirements on energy-related US origin items, and determined a vigorous reply from the European Union, in a time when the Trans-Siberian pipeline was being built (with an important participation of British, French, German and Italian firms) to supply the continent with natural gas.[20]

In August 1982, the European Commission and the Danish Presidency of the Council of the European Union, sent a memorandum of protest to the US administration, highlighting that "*the US regulations contain sweeping extensions of US jurisdiction which are unlawful under international law*", that "*goods and technology do not have any nationality*", but also that "*the statutory encouragement of voluntary submission to US public policy in trade matters within the EC is strongly condemned* [As a result of] *the inclusion of submission clauses in private contracts, freedom of contracts is misused in order to circumvent the limits imposed on national jurisdiction by international law*".[21]

The end of those restrictive measures had the effect to mitigate the controversy. However, the EU continued to refuse extra-territorial enforcement via Council Regulation 2271/96 and Joint Action 96/668/CFSP.

Regulation No 2271/96,[22] in particular, stated that whenever a person's economic and/or financial interest are affected by the extraterritorial application of legislation adopted in a third country, the Commission shall be informed within 30 days from the date on which such information was obtained.[23] However, in 1997, the European Union and the United States reached an agreement by which the effects of this regulation were essentially "frozen". As a result, at present the EU legal system does not contain, neither at European or Member State's level, any specific provision to counter extraterritorial effects in the field of export controls.[24]

7.5 Implementation by Economic Operators: Effects and "Side Effects"

Although not legally binding in the European Union, from the point of view of exporters, compliance with US regulation is inevitable.

[20]Q. Genard, *cit.*, p. 7.

[21]Comments of the European Community on the Amendments of 22 June 1982 to the US Export Control Regulations, 12 August 1982, US-EC Dispute Over the Gas Pipeline from Siberia to Western Europe. Available: http://aei.pitt.edu/1768/1/US_dispute_comments_1982.pdf.

[22]Council Regulation (EC) No 2271/96 of 22 November 1996 protecting against the effects of the extra-territorial application of legislation adopted by a third country, and actions based thereon or resulting therefrom, Official Journal L 309, 29/11/1996 pp. 0001–0006.

[23]Council Regulation (EC) No 2271/96 of 22 November 1996, *cit.*, art. 2.

[24]Q. Michel, S. Paile, *cit.*, p. 73.

Corporate interests need to protect their businesses, avoid sanctions, protect their reputation, and guarantee their ability to maintain their supply chain and be able to participate to public procurement tenders.

If no country or company wants to be proscribed by such an essential market, taking into account the lack of foreign availability of certain technologies and the consequent risk for the security of supply, the active enforcement of violations outside of the US has received a lot of attention and made compliance with such regulations an utmost priority.

The main target has been financial institutions, as they play a very central role in trade-related transactions (in October 2015, French Crédit Agricole agreed to pay $787 M penalty for allegedly processing transactions that violated US sanctions related to Iran, Sudan, Cuba and Myanmar, succeeding BNP Paribas that pleaded guilty to criminal charges and paid a record $8.9bn penalty; in 2012, ING Bank N.V., headquartered in the Netherlands, agreed to pay 619 million $, not much less had had to pay in the previous years ABN AMRO Bank N.V., now Royal Bank of Scotland (RBS)($500 million, 2010), Barclays Bank ($298 million, 2010), Credit Suisse ($536 million, 2009), and Lloyds TSB Bank ($350 million, 2009).

However, other sectors have been impacted, such as aeronautics (Fokker, Netherlands, in 2015), but also chemical and agricultural products (Chemical Partners, Belgium, in 2016).

Private entities have witnessed that US export control violations not only can lead to severe fines and criminal or civil sanctions, but also to loss of market shares, ban from receiving any US items, and important reputational damage both for companies and managers. In 2012, French aeronautics spare parts company Aerotechnics France was accused to have illegally exported US military items to Iran: the names of the company and of its CEO were added to the Entity List. When a new company was created from it, with a new managerial board, the Commerce Department evidenced a direct nexus with the previous company and listed the new firm and CEO as well. Only more recently the names were finally taken off the list.[25]

When dealing with items or technology that are controlled under US export control laws, it is therefore important that European exporters know that compliance obligations might be attached to their procurement and re-export, fully understand the regulations and set up effective compliance programs. This being said, the extra-territorial application may determine potential "side effects" and conflicts of regulations where the private entity may be confronted with a lack of official guidance by the national government and will de facto experience forms of competitive disadvantage or even need to weigh the risk of non compliance against conflicting regulations.

[25]Department of Commerce, Bureau of Industry and Security, Addition of Certain Persons to the Entity List and Implementation of the Entity List Annual Review Changes, Federal Register Volume 77, No 25, April 2012.

7.6 Effects and "Side Effects" of the Implementation of Export Control Requirements

It has been already mentioned how critical it is for European businesses to integrate multi-layered compliance requirements in their internal compliance schemes.

At the same time, the implementation of trade restriction may expose the company to adverse effects such as potential conflicts of regulations, distortions of competition and un-level playing field between big businesses and Small and Medium Enterprises (SMEs).

If several sets of rules are enforced nationally as well as extra-territorially, the first consequence for the economic operator is that compliance is a fixed cost. Important investments are generally required to achieve a "mistake-proof" internal compliance program, through extensive training, screening database services, and sophisticated IT systems to ensure all controls are carried out before the shipment of hardware. In this sense, the ability to abide by certain standards resides—in all or in part-in the capacity to finance the necessary investments, with a consequent dis-proprortion between big businesses and SMEs.

Also, the licensing-related administrative burden naturally leads to asymmetries between a US and a non-US company, with potential effects on their equal ability to compete on the global market.

A US license will be needed in order to procure and re-export hardware, but also in order to work on a project involving technology originated on the other side of the Atlantic, whenever an employee of nationality different from the country of incorporation is involved and whenever a non-US sub-contractor is involved: in this sense, additional costs, risks and delays will need to be taken into account by a company located outside of the US.

On the other hand for hardware transiting through the US, imported in the US or in order to work on a US technology-related project, no particular authorization will be required for a "domestic" company, incorporated in the US and whose employees are all US citizens or green-card holders (in which case, it becomes irrelevant whether the person holds additional nationalities or was born in a third country).

While US regulations are integrated in the compliance schemes of any European company, it may be questioned whether extraterritorial enforcement is consistent with international law principles as well as with explicit prohibitions related to extra-territorial enforcement and contained in certain sources of EU law. A company may thus, in specific cases, ultimately have to decide with which regulation to comply and which one to breach, based on a risk assessment which is generally favorable to the ones that are more actively enforced.

Living up to US laws may conflict with EU provisions in certain circumstances. EU directives on anti-discrimination (with minor variations in the wording incorporated in the implementation texts in each Member State) prohibit discrimination based on nationality, at the same title as other forms of discriminations, based on gender, religion, or political orientation.

On the other hand, complying with US "deemed re-export" regulations inevitably entails specific restrictions on employees holding citizenship of a third country or multiple nationalities. While in some cases such restrictions may be waived by the obtention of an appropriate license, for some others there is presumption of denial. Interestingly, a EU Member State results as "blacklisted" under ITAR §126.1, Cyprus. Should a European company open a job position, or start working on a program where US technology needs to be accessed, there is a risk of conflict between the injunction of the US legislator, that prescribes not to give access to individuals born in Cyprus or holding nationality of this country, unless they are US citizens, and the prohibition under national laws not to discriminate on the basis of nationality, notably between "European citizens".

The end-result may be excluding certain job candidates based on their nationality or not being able to offer the same opportunities to employees with different nationalities in projects including US technology. While in some cases European companies have offered compensations to those employees that they could not allow working on such projects, these practices may expose companies to lawsuits with a high probability of success, since economic considerations cannot justify unequal treatment and US regulations cannot be invoked as exclusive justification since they are not legally binding in the EU.

Although some of the most recent political development may lead to foresee a future change in foreign policy vis-à-vis countries such as Iran or Cuba, the United States maintain special restrictions on countries subject to arms embargoes that go above and beyond the decisions taken by the UN Security Council under Chapter VII and therefore what is legally binding for all States. These political decisions may not necessarily be shared by the European Union, like in the case of Cuba.

When dealing with countries such as Russia, Iran or Cuba, Regulation 2271/1996/EU (directly applicable to all EU member states) in its art. 5 prohibit companies to live up to the extraterritorial regulations, explicitly referring to US laws (National Defense Authorization Act, Cuban Liberty and Democratic Solidarity Act, Iran and Libya sanctions act). While there is a possibility to apply for an exception with the European Commission, until today this option has never been utilized and the "blocking statute" in practice has never been enforced. As mentioned earlier, this may nevertheless be invoked in case of lawsuit and would not find sufficient legal justification in compliance with US laws which extra-territorial application is explicitly prohibited in the EU.

Side effects may concern also a more and more "sensitive" topic in Europe: data protection. In the most recent years, and especially with the incredible growth of the use of internet and the social media, several European authorities started to wonder whether the use and "marketing" of European personal data is consistent with EU law.

The recent decision by the EU Court of Justice[26] on the Safe Harbor Agreement and the current development of a "EU-US Data Privacy Shield" is evidence that European courts and public authorities are starting to see the legal conditions imposed by the US more and more critically and are openly starting to challenge their extra-territorial scope.

US regulations may go beyond the UN Security Council decisions by issuing additional lists of sanctioned entities and denied parties. However under EU law, no reference to "screening" is made and it is unsure whether use of personal data to this aim can be acceptable without prior consent.

Any use or handling of personal data and screening in the EU need to be justified, at the risk of being considered as illegal. However, given that employers which fail to carry out data synchronisation may be punished; it may be considered that there is a legitimate interest in carrying out data screening.[27]

In case of lawsuit, compliance with US laws would not be sufficient justification, and even where it is authorized via explicit consent, in certain jurisdictions, like in Germany, the latter may be deemed as invalid if required in a context of hierarchy or position of influence. As of today, different courts have expressed diverging views over screening, notably in relation to the acquisition of the certification of "Authorized Economic Operator".[28]

Extraterritoriality may also entail distortion of competition: it has been already mentioned how different can be the business environment for American companies dealing with US products on the territory of the United States, and similar or identical companies located abroad, notably when the items concerned are ITAR classified. *A minima* multiple regulatory requirements apply to the firm located in the US, with duplicative requirements, potential conflicts, but also an inevitable reduction of customer and supplier choice, with consequent distortion of competition. This has been highlighted also in other domains, such as financial services in particular with reference to US anti-trust law.

7.7 Conclusions

If extra-territorial enforcement of US export control regulations on the territory of other States has been subject to debate in the European Union since the early 1980s, it is today a requirement in any internal compliance programme of companies that

[26]Court of Justice of the European Union, PRESS RELEASE No 117/15, Luxembourg, 6 October 2015, Judgment in Case C-362/14, Maximillian Schrems v Data Protection Commissioner. Available: http://curia.europa.eu/jcms/upload/docs/application/pdf/2015-10/cp150117en.pdf.

[27]International Law Office, "Anti-terrorism regulations: co-determination and data protection", 22 June 2011. Available: http://www.internationallawoffice.com/Newsletters/Employment-Benefits/Germany/CMS-Hasche-Sigle/Anti-terrorism-regulations-co-determination-and-data-protection.

[28]See for instance: Squire Patton Boggs, "Anti-Terrorist screening obligations: Employers on the Horns of a Dilemma", 2014, http://www.squirepattonboggs.com/~/media/files/insights/publications/2015/01/anti-terror-2/antiterrorscreeningsalert.pdf.

although legally incorporated in Europe, procure items, receive technical data and cooperate with international partners on programs including US technology or that are by-products of US technologies.

The addition of the extra-territorial enforcement of US export control regulations to national requirements nevertheless may determine "contradictory obligations" on a legal entity.[29] Whenever potential conflicts arise, fear of sanctions from the US (systematically enforced, widely communicated and publicly accessible, with the risk of being blacklisted, and the threat of steep pecuniary sanctions) need to be weighted against local regulations, often preventive in nature and less actively enforced. In this sense, the implementation of export controls requirements for an economic actor on the market that deals with controlled US-origin technology exposes companies to risks that are often not conforted by a specific guidance by the national authorities.

In this sense, harmonization and the establishment of some form of mutual recognition or comparability is essential, to prevent burdensome analysis of multiple requirements, obtain clear guidance when local law and extraterritorial provisions may be potentially conflicting or incompatible and eliminate secondary effects such as the establishment of an unlevel playing field with restricted choices in terms of customers, suppliers and business partners in general, with potential effects on the whole supply chain.

---

[29]B.Stern, *cit.*, p. 15.

Chapter 8
BOTTICELLI Project: Enhancing Export Control Cooperation Between Industry and Governments

Sandro Zero and Alejandra Charpentier

Abstract Considering the important role of the Industry in this process, for the tenth anniversary of the 1540 resolution on the November 2014 Wiesbaden meeting in Frankfurt, industry was invited by the 1540 Committee, the German and the US Governments, UNODA and the European Commission, to take a greater role in contributing to the non-proliferation regime by strengthening the effective application of export controls. The BOTTICELLI Project was created as an answer to this invitation; the initiative confirms the industrial determination to actively contribute to international stability, peace and security by supporting governments in the implementation of the 1540 Resolution. This Project promotes an Export Control Culture, common Export Control Principles and smart practices without distortion of the competition.

Keywords BOTTICELLI · The 1540 resolution · The 1540 committee

8.1 Introduction

Since the creation of the first nuclear weapon, the international community faces the threat of proliferation of weapons of mass destruction. States are therefore conscious that there must be a strict control and a global commitment of the nuclear suppliers and exporters. 190 States have ratified the Non Proliferation Treaty whose aim is to counter the risk of proliferation while at the same time promoting the positive civil use of nuclear energy.

The 9/11 events radically changed the notion of international security, terrorism threat became global increasing the concerns of proliferation.

The idea of weapons of mass destruction ending up in terrorist hands is an extremely dangerous scenario that must be avoided by all means. Indeed in 2004 the United Nations Security Council adopted the Resolution 1540 which aims at

S. Zero (✉) · A. Charpentier
AREVA, Courbevoie, France
e-mail: sandro.zero@studiozero.fr; sandro.zero@areva.com

D. Tamada and P. Achilleas (eds.), *Theory and Practice of Export Control*,
Kobe University Social Science Research Series,
DOI 10.1007/978-981-10-5960-5_8

impeding non-state actors to acquire any sensitive material that could be used to produce and deliver weapons of mass destruction (WMD).

The 1540 Resolution imposes binding obligations on all member States of the United Nations and is addressed to governments establishing the provisions that States must respect in order to avoid terrorist actors obtaining access to chemical, biological and nuclear materials including their means of delivery.

Nevertheless, as proliferation is a worldwide concern the fight against it should not be only a government's duty but a global one where all actors of the civil society and particularly industries shall involve and contribute to the non-proliferation regime.

Industries indeed, are conscious to be the first barrier against proliferation, they know their products, their markets and clients, what are the risks, challenges and the possible ways to address them; for instance their engagement in the Export Control Programs and their expertise would be an advantageous tool to succeed in this common goal.

Considering the important role of the Industry in this process, for the tenth anniversary of the 1540 resolution on the November 2014 Wiesbaden meeting in Frankfurt, industry was invited by the 1540 Committee, the German and the US Governments, UNODA and the European Commission, to take a greater role in contributing to the non-proliferation regime by strengthening the effective application of export controls.

The BOTTICELLI Project was created as an answer to this invitation; the initiative confirms the industrial determination to actively contribute to international stability, peace and security by supporting governments in the implementation of the 1540 Resolution.

This Project promotes an Export Control Culture, common Export Control Principles and smart practices without distortion of the competition.

8.2 BOTTICELLI Project: Addressing Nowadays Needs and Challenges

In a context of international tensions, the proliferation risk could impede the harmonious trade and development of sensitive goods for civil applications.

The nature of dual-use goods and technology makes the export of these products subject to strict controls under national, regional and international regulations. However, different regulation systems are developing two main concerns:

On one hand, the systematic increase of procedures adds a barrier to the effective control and withdraws attention, energy and resources from real risks;

On the other hand, different regulations or different interpretation of the same regulation can affect the level playing field and thus distort competition.

The clarification, harmonization and simplification of international rules and practices would reduce the risk of proliferation allowing becoming more effective in the prevention of illicit trafficking and proliferation.

The BOTTICELLI Project considers establishing a common set of international export practices for suppliers of dual-use goods and controlled technologies by proposing Ten Export Control Principles to commit to.

This initiative is a worldwide non-profit association chaired by a Group of international Experts inside a sound organization composed by a Secretariat, Sectors, Members and Supporting Members.

The scope is organized in Sectors and composed by the three sensitive sectors at risk for possibly contributing to the Weapons of Mass Destruction (Biology, Chemistry, Nuclear) and their four delivery sectors: Aerospace, Information Technology, Transport and Finance.

Members (Exporters from the Industry, Research Centers and Academia) are direct suppliers of dual-use products and thus, belong to the seven sectors previously mentioned. They expressly commit to the Ten Principles which have been directly inspired from the 1540 Resolution with the scope of enhancing export security.

Supporting members (Governments, Associations and Institutions) do not commit to the Ten Principles as they are not exporters and are not linked to sensitive goods but they share the same values and objectives of the Members and support them in their missions.

The BOTTICELLI Project aims at promoting cooperation between Members and Supporting Members with the scope of:

- Confirming industry's determination to contribute to the fight against proliferation of weapons of mass destruction.
- Supporting the efforts of the international community in the implementation of the UNSCR 1540.
- Promoting efficient and smart practices used by the most compliant sectors.
- Facilitating access by customer and partner countries to dual-use goods, controlled technologies and associated services.
- Increasing awareness among Members to understand proliferation mechanisms and the ways to counter them, creating a real Export Control Culture.
- Avoiding diversion of attention from the real risks in order to become more effective in terms of export security whilst facilitating positive and constructive commercial trade.
- Engaging industry in the export control system.
- Enhancing legal and regulatory frameworks and the capacity of authorities to implement a common minimum regulatory baseline.

In order to achieve the above objectives, BOTTICELLI Project participants will contribute to the following series of deliverables:

- A reference set of industry export control guidelines and smart practices
- A reference Internal Compliance Program
- A reference Self-Assessment and a roster of experts
- The promotion of the Project to new members and the conduction of self-assessments and peer reviews.

In addition, the initiative foresees a number of guidelines included in a three section program:

The first section presents the "**Ten Principles of Conduct**" that members commit to.

The second section "**Comply with the current system**" presents the operational practices that the industry implements today in order to comply with the existing regulations.

The third section "**Towards an effective system**" responds to the new evolving of the international market and proposes an export control organization ready to adapt to the new challenges thanks to a risk based approach model.

The wording "**Export Monitoring**" instead of "**Export Control**" would better reflect the cooperation between the industry and the regulators with this new approach.

8.3 The Ten Principles of Conduct

This section presents the commitment of the industry to the fundamental Principles of the Export Control which directly refer to the 1540 Resolution articles.

Members adhere to the Project on a voluntary basis with the intention of expressly committing to the Ten Principles which entail many advantages:

- Efficient, clear and relevant export control principles will avoid risk diversion and reduce the proliferation threat whilst allowing the positive civilian application of Dual Use products and technologies.
- Engaging the major international industries working on Dual-Use products as well as their partners and supply chain to commit to the Ten Principles will guarantee that all exporters of strategic products and technologies contribute to enhance global security.
- While recalling common principles, the initiative also ensures authorities and customers (potential or confirmed) that projects will be achieved on time and in Compliance with export regulations.
- The Ten Principles, directly inspired from the 1540 Resolution and acceptable worldwide promote an Export Control Culture across industries which will allow governments to focus their attention and resources on exports that pose the greatest risks.
- The fight against proliferation should impede the use of sensitive material to illegal means and not be an element of distortion of the competition. A non-proliferation legal system transparent, solid and common to Exporters will be a source of inspiration for the rest of the world and would enable effectively to address this threat.
- By committing to the Ten Principles, industry demonstrates its willingness to create and implement a high standard of transparency, integrity, ethical behavior

and social responsibility in compliance with laws and regulations which will enhance public acceptance.

- The ten Principles will allow the BOTTICELLI Project to become a common industry reference for any Internal Compliance and Outreach Program.

8.4 The Ten Principles of Conduct

I **Refrain from providing any form of support** to any individual or entity that attempts, contrary to applicable export control laws, to develop, acquire, manufacture, possess, transport, transfer or use nuclear, chemical or biological weapons and their means of delivery.

II **Create and enforce an effective Internal Compliance Program (ICP)** that includes a commitment from the highest level of Member management, procedures, dedicated export control officers (ECO), and training, as well as self-assessments and/or audits and extend the foregoing to each Member's suppliers, sub-contractors and to the supply chain.

III **Develop** effective **protection measures and provide funds and services to account and secure** sensitive items in production, use, storage, transport, transit, trans-shipment, re-export and control, as well as establishing end-user controls.

IV **Support the establishment of a sound structure** of the BOTTICELLI Project composed of a Secretariat and the following Sectors: Aerospace, Chemical, Biology, Nuclear, Information technology, Transport and Finance; aimed at recommending appropriate effective procedures and guidelines consistent with applicable export control laws.

V **Interpret** this list of Principles consistently with the rights and obligations arising under applicable export control laws.

VI **Establish a list** of products, material, technology, services, training and technical assistance that are subject to applicable export control laws and to yearly pursue the update of such lists.

VII **Offer** assistance as appropriate in response to specific requests to other exporters in order to implement the provisions of these Principles.

VIII **Promote the universal adoption** and full implementation of these Principles.

IX **Promote dialogue and cooperation** between industry, academia, research centers, national and international institutions and governments.

X **Monitor closely the implementation** of these Principles through regular peer reviews and by other agreed upon means.

8.5 Comply with the Current System

This section presents the operational practice of the industry in order to comply with current regulations. Cooperation between industries, regulators and international institutions will respond to current needs of the international market concerning large international projects and the modern organization of the supply chain.

The current regulations indeed, are more adapted to punctual bilateral exports of tangible goods while there are an increasing number of operations concerning tangible and intangible supplies for large projects over a longer period of time.

(1) **Promoting general licenses for dual-use goods**

General licenses allow movements for dual-use goods in certain regions. Thus, they rationalize the regulation related to export control and reinforce the stability of the markets.

(2) **Free movement between subsidiaries of a same company**

Subsidiaries working for the same firm are required to demand an individual license if they want to exchange dual-use goods and technology.

This provision is not adapted to the current business world because, on one hand businesses have internationalized their teams; and on the other intangible technology is commonly transferred through shared servers.

An exemption of export licenses for intra-company operations would be smart and beneficial for companies having in place a qualified ICP.

(3) **Technology exports by universities or research centers**

Questions are often raised concerning the necessity of controlling technology produced by universities and research centers.

The latter claims it is their duty to share their knowledge with the general public and for instance they consider not to be concerned by Export Control rules.

On the contrary, industries consider technology exports of research centers, universities and industries to be equally sensitive and thus, subject to the same controls concerning dual-use regulations. It is in fact the dual-use nature to which technology refers and not the legal status of the exporter that should be considered.

Technology transfers remain a sensitive issue whether it is produced by industries, universities or research centers; for instance a differentiation has no justification in terms of non-proliferation and would be damaging for the industry.

A possible solution would be to establish a technology threshold above which a license would be required.

(4) **Ensuring a control of the Intangible Technology by an ICP and an auditable Authorized Economic Operator of companies**

Technology is usually exported by intangible means.

Dual-Use technology requires an export license delivered by industries' national authorities. Because of the intangible nature of the export, the license will not be submitted to the customs like it would be the case for tangible Dual-Use products. As a result, it is the exporter who has the responsibility of booking the license and keeping track of the exportation in order to keep his exports reporting up to date and in conformity with the export license.

Nevertheless, this practice has no legal explicit obligation, so the only way to inform exporters how to carry out a control over intangible exports and ensure their legality would be the Internal Compliance Program (ICP).

The ICP, as the Authorized Economic Operator (AEO) would be auditable, but they should constitute a real benefit in terms of export facilitation.

(5) **Human Rights approach in the Dual-Use items regulation**

It is necessary to keep in mind the priority goal of the Export Control which is the non-proliferation of weapons of mass destruction. Human Rights should be addressed within an «ad hoc» and more appropriate framework, the concept is relatively vague and complex and differs from the original scope of the Export Control.

Human Rights should not be considered as a criterion in Export Control because it will not contribute to the non-proliferation efforts as it will increase the administrative burden already difficult to implement. At the same time, the concept of Human Rights will not be served as needed either.

(6) **Cooperation between Industry and Government in the implementation of a «unique» international regulation**

Industries are directly concerned by Export Control rules and their adherence and compliance with them is of paramount importance to ensure collective success.

Being the first ones on the ground and having the capacity to identify deficiencies and understand the challenges concerning their products, industrials can contribute with their view and expertise to the implementation of measures related to the export control.

For instance, an active and dynamic dialogue between Industry and Governments would be advantageous to allow a faster reaction, adaptation and update of lists of dual-use products in order to better take into account a rapid development of technology.

If the industry could easily report its needs to the Government and international institutions, it would be easier to optimize the security of information transfers and enhance the effectiveness of the worldwide system.

(7) **International Advisory Committee for Industry (IACI) exporting DU items**

International DU regimes are represented by various intergovernmental groups, such as the Nuclear Suppliers Group (NSG), WASSENAAR, MTCR, AUSTRALIA Group or the 1540 Committee. Nevertheless, there is no representation of the industry in such regimes.

A consulting group of enterprises similar to other existing groups would be useful and beneficial in order to listen the concerns and points of view of the Industry when it comes to dual-use goods. Recalling the principle of cooperation and dialogue, this Industrial Committee could give advices to decision-making bodies and propose possible solutions to the challenges found on the ground. The current existing body at the European level is the Dual Use Group of Business Europe which is the leading voice of European enterprises.

The BOTTICELLI Project has the elements needed to become the industry's representative.

(8) **License exemptions (or export facilitation) to countries and entities being themselves exporters of DU items**

The scope of export licenses is to counter the risk of proliferation of dual-use goods. The export of products and technologies to States or entities that do not possess those products or technologies clearly justifies a strict control and export licenses.

On the contrary, most of the time, exports are made between States or entities that already possess the knowledge of the technologies exported. Such exports are made for contractual and economic reasons; for instance, demanding licenses for this kind of exports do not contribute to the non-proliferation goal. Instead, they delay the procedures and add complexities to the licit export operations while withdrawing time, budget and workforce from exports that constitute real risks.

(9) **Mutual recognition of Export Control systems in the world**

In the absence of a unique international regulation and in the same spirit of administrative rationalization, regulation and simplification; a mutual recognition at the international level of the quality and effectiveness of the export control systems would ensure dynamism of exchanges and would facilitate exports. These «mutual recognitions», based on trust (and EC outreach) between States, would avoid duplicate export control procedures and would be based on the robustness of effective export control systems.

Extraterritoriality of the national law should be avoided.

(10) **Facilitation for licensing of spare parts or license renewal**

A significant number of exports concern the supply of spare parts. When a license has been delivered for the original component, why would exporters need to repeat the licensing procedure to export a justified replacement part?

The industry's experience, certified by and AEO and an ICP must enable the assessment of the client's need and the relevance of supplying a spare part.

(11) **Implementation of symmetric practices**

Ending asymmetric practices between countries would allow a level playing field and an easier implementation of mutual recognitions.

(12) **Introduction of «de minimis» for no sensitive items**

The current Dual-Use regulation considers exports of sensitive materials subject to the same controls with no distinction between an exportation of a few tons of controlled materials and an exportation of very small quantities of products. Introducing a «de minimis rule» could facilitate exchanges while maintaining an effective control.

(13) **Catch-All clause and license denial**

A Catch-all clause should be used to control products not explicitly listed in the regulations. In order to alert other countries of the new risks, the catch-all decision should be communicated to an international body (1540 Committee) which will be in charge of communicating the catch-all decision worldwide.

This should also be the case when it comes to a license denial. In order to fix the dysfunction, exporters should report every catch-all or license denial to an international body (UN 1540 Committee).

8.6 Towards an Effective System

This section proposes an export control organization based on an effective product/country risk of proliferation (risk approach model) and a reference international regulation able to prevent any interpretation of the regulations and any distortion of the competition. This model will be more adapted to the current industrial practice and new challenges and will enhance the effective fight against proliferation.

The export control system, rather than a constraint to the industry, will be an effective tool to counter proliferation of WMD and protect industry without interfering with the day-to-day commerce.

(1) **Risk-based approach**

The concept of «risk-based approach» is linked to the «smart security approach». Currently, all products listed on the regulation lists are subject to the same controls without any distinction related to the different levels of proliferation risk.

Moreover, the regulations do not take into consideration neither the State-user, nor the final beneficiary of the export. As a result, whether a dual-use product is exported within the same region (EU), outside the region or even to a sensitive country, the export procedure will be administrated in the same way. This means that, while exports that represent more risk will be treated the same way than those that don't, products and countries representing less risk will be penalized with an unnecessary increase in the burden of procedures.

A possible solution would be that each industry proposes to governments a list of products with a proliferation risk associated while governments propose to industries a list of sensitive countries.

Hereafter is an example of scheme for a possible «risk-based approach» specific for the nuclear sector:

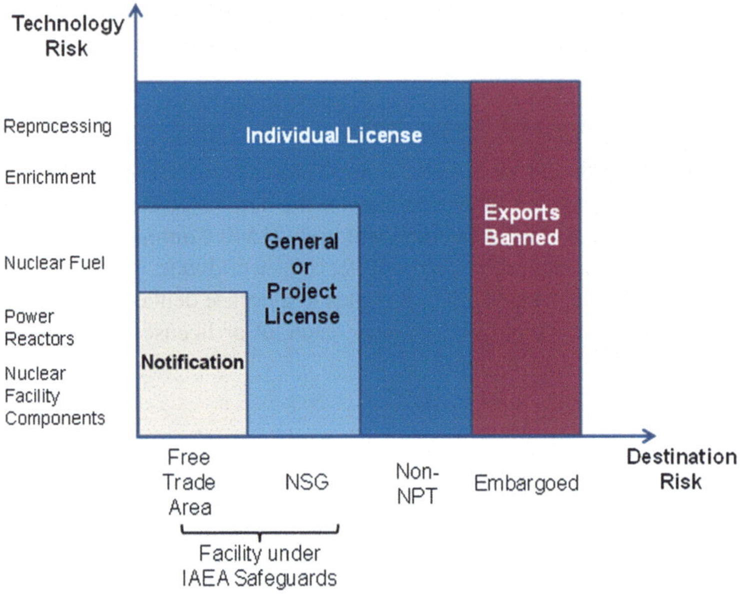

(2) **Necessity of a unique license for Large (long) Projects**

Currently in France as well as in the European Union (Regulation 428/2009), individual export licenses duration is limited to two years. As a result, to complete a «large project» many export licenses, including the ones by the main contract holder, its subsidiaries and subcontractors are required. In contrast, the US regulation requires only one export license valid for the whole scope and duration of the project. Considering that customers take today into consideration the administrative burdens when choosing their supplier, this gives the US a significant competitive advantage compared to the burden of European procedures inside and outside the EU.

In addition, in the case of a Large Project, the client-country may impose some local suppliers who would also be beneficiaries of the exports. A license adapted to large projects which should last the same duration of the project would insure a level playing field and avoid the distortion of competition.

A unique license, for various identified countries of destination, for series of components and associated technologies, for a series of users and valid for the expected duration of a project, would be more adapted to Large Projects carried out abroad.

(3) **From an Export Control System to an Export Monitoring System**

The purpose of the Export Control System is to preserve exports of listed products from a possible use for illegal means. As previously mentioned, the current export control organization has an impact on delivery delays and distortion of the competition. As a result, exporters may see the Export Control System as a burden rather than added value securing their exports.

Upgrading the current system by moving from a «control system» to a «monitoring system» while promoting cooperation between concerned actors will allow exporters see the Export Control System as an ally rather than as a constraint.

(4) **A unique and clear international regulation to prevent distortions of competition. Extension of the level-playing field to the EU and to the world (*urbi et orbi*)**

Proliferation has no borders and is a common and global concern. Therefore, it must be addressed collectively on an equal basis and without exceptions by all countries: those possessing the nuclear weapon and those which do not, by large and small countries, by Northern and Southern ones, by rich and poor countries.

This common concern needs to be addressed by all under the same common rules (Unique International Regulation, INFCIRC 254 for example) preventing distortion of the competition and flaws in the systems likely to benefit violators.

Very often, a same regulation can be differently interpreted and implemented ine different countries and even inside a same country, by different administrations.

Common supranational good practices, unquestionable and clear applicable to everyone in a standardized and coherent way would be the solution to this asymmetric respect of rules.

Unique procedure, unique license, same conditions and documents to obtain a license, same warranties, same validity of the license respectable by all exporters without leaving place to interpretation.

A unique regulation and a unique implementation would harmonize practices of all States and thus, increase motivation of exporters to develop an Export Control (Monitoring) Culture while eradicating the possibility of distorting competition or diverting controls.

8.7 Conclusion

Sensitive products for civil applications are part of our daily needs. Unfortunately, these products can also be used to create weapons of mass destruction. Proliferation of dual-use materials can be a threat to international peace and security. As a result, governments and international institutions have drafted strict laws and regulations in order to secure and control the exportation of such products. The current situation demonstrates that, even if regulations have proved to be efficient, the rapid evolution of technology and the emergence of new challenges require regulations to be adapted and improved.

Proliferation is not only a government's issue. Industry is equally affected and concerned. In addition, industry being in the first line against proliferation, can bring an advantageous element to support governments enhance export security. Cooperative action between industries and decision-makers is of paramount importance to enhance the efficiency of any Export Control system.

The BOTTICELLI Project is a worldwide association aiming to make this cooperative action possible. It proves the determination of exporters to actively contribute to international security and responds to UNODA's call for industries to take an active role in the non-proliferation regime.

By enhancing dialogue and cooperation between governments and industry, the export control system will be better prepared to face emerging challenges (intangible transfers, 3D manufacturing, new technologies, e-commerce) and focus on exports that constitute the greatest risk. As a result, the fight against proliferation and illicit trafficking will be effectively strengthened without distorting the competition. A global commitment of institutions, governments and industry is the key to collectively succeeding against proliferation and terrorism.

Part III
Export Control in Relevant Areas of International Law

Chapter 9
Conflict of Interests: Liberalisation of Foreign Direct Investment Versus Security Interest

Dai Tamada

Abstract This article focuses on the conflict between the economic interest and the security interest which has appeared in the recent Free Trade Agreements (FTA). In the investment chapter, the FTA tends to admit the liberalisation of foreign direct investment (FDI) and this can endanger the security interest of host-States. Thus, FTA contains several clauses which limit the liberalisation of FDI, for the purpose of balancing the two interests. This article is aimed at showing the legal techniques of this balancing in one of the most recent FTAs, i.e. Trans-Pacific Partnership Agreement (TPP).

Keywords FTA · Foreign direct investment · Security exception · TPP

9.1 Introduction

Export control stems from the necessity of non-proliferation of military or dual goods. It is thus reasonable to think that it relates mainly to the restriction of trade and commerce, which are embodied in the principle of free trade. On this point, it can be safely said that the conflict of interest between trade and security has always been resolved in favour of the latter (i.e. in the interest of peace and security). In fact, the General Agreement on Tariffs and Trade (GATT), the World Trade Organization (WTO) agreements, free trade agreements (FTAs), and economic partnership agreements (EPAs) normally contain exception clauses, which admit the restriction of trade in exceptional cases, namely, in the presence of international security concerns. For instance, an embargo in the form of economic sanctions in conformity with resolutions of the Security Council of the United Nations does not constitute a breach of treaties which contain the exception clause.

On the other hand, the scope of international economic law, which can be in conflict with security interests, is not limited to the traditional notion of 'trade', but

D. Tamada (✉)
Graduate School of Law, Kobe University, Osaka, Japan
e-mail: tamada@port.kobe-u.ac.jp

D. Tamada and P. Achilleas (eds.), *Theory and Practice of Export Control*,
Kobe University Social Science Research Series,
DOI 10.1007/978-981-10-5960-5_9

we should take into account the law of investment, especially that of foreign direct investment (FDI). This is because security interests can conflict with the transfer of money. Thus, in this chapter, we examine the conflict of interests between the liberalisation of FDI and security interests.

In brief, the liberalisation of FDI basically means that countries, which are the contracting parties to particular treaties, have to open their domestic markets, including several sensitive sectors like the nuclear energy, aircraft, telecommunication sectors, and so on, to foreign investors. In such a case, the security interest, *stricto* sensu, is not the only thing at stake; the issue also touches upon economic security in general.

In this chapter, we follow the traditional regulation of FDI pertaining to security interests in the form of an exception clause included in L'Organisation Européenne de Coopération Économique (OECE) Code (2). This stance has been maintained by recent international agreements. Moreover, it is necessary to examine the more developed style of regulation on conflict of interests. For this purpose, we refer to the exception clause and the non-conforming measures (NCM) clause of the Trans-Pacific Partnership Agreement (TPP) (3). Lastly, it is also necessary to review the domestic regulation. To do so, we select, as an example, the Foreign Trade Act of Japan, which controls inward FDI on the basis of security interests (4).

9.2 Exception Clause in the OECD Code of Liberalisation of Capital Movements

It is necessary to confirm the fundamental rules pertaining to direct foreign investment regulations. *First*, States are not obliged under customary international law to admit/receive inward direct investments. In other words, States are free to regulate or prohibit a substantial portion of foreign investment or to exclude foreign investment from several of their sensitive industries. *Second*, on the contrary, there is a tendency for International Investment Agreements (IIAs) to protect, promote, and even liberalise FDI. When a State enters into such treaties, including FTAs, EPAs, IIAs, and Bilateral Investment Treaties (BITs), they have to admit, receive, and protect foreign investment.

This trend dates back to the OECD Code of Liberalisation of Capital Movements (OECD/C(61)96).[1] In 1960, the Council of the OECD adopted the decision called the *Code of Liberalisation of Capital Movements* (which entered into force in 1961).[2] It provided a balanced framework for countries to progressively remove

[1]The OECD Code of Liberalisation of Capital Movements (OECD/C(61)96). Available at [http://www.oecd.org/daf/inv/investment-policy/CapitalMovements_WebEnglish.pdf].

[2]This decision shall be called the Code. See Article 21 of the Code. It should be noted that the decisions of the OECD Council are legally binding. This differs from recommendations, declarations, and guidelines.

barriers to the movement of capital, while providing flexibility to cope with situations of economic and financial instability. Although the Code basically aims to liberalise capital movement among the contracting States, it admits some exceptions. Article 3 (Public Order and Security) provides the following.

The provisions of this Code shall not prevent a Member from taking action which it considers necessary for:

(i) the maintenance of public order or the protection of public health, morals, and safety;
(ii) the protection of its essential security interests; and
(iii) the fulfilment of its obligations relating to international peace and security.

As is shown here, while the Code admits the principal need of liberalisation of investment (free movement of capital), it allows several exceptions on the bases of public order, essential security, and international peace and security. This idea has been maintained by other relevant treaties on the protection and liberalisation of investment.

9.3 Balance Between Investment and Security in International Law

The potential for conflict between investment and security has never disappeared, and indeed, this situation has only worsened. Since the FTAs tend to develop and promote the protection and liberalisation of FDI more deeply and widely than before, the conflict between these two interests has become increasingly severe. The TPP,[3] one of mega FTAs, is a good example for examining how the contracting parties have resolved the issue of balance between investment and security. This is because they purport to substantially increase the openness of their own markets to foreign investors (i.e. via liberalisation of investment). As we see below, the TPP has an aspect of liberalisation of investment (3.1). This means that the contracting parties have to open their markets to foreign investors/investments. Against this, the TPP contains two exception clauses and relevant annexes. The first is the General Exception clause applicable to the case of protecting security interests (3.2). The second case refers to the clause and annexes concerning the non-conforming measures which exempt the contracting states from applying the liberalisation clause (3.3).

[3]The official text of the TPP (adopted on 26 January 2016) is available at [http://tpp.mfat.govt.nz/text].

9.3.1 Liberalisation of Investment Under the TPP

It is quite important to know that the investment chapter of the TPP is aimed not only at the *protection* of investment, but also at its *liberalisation*. The 'liberalisation', in this context, means that the contracting parties have to admit and receive the inward FDI into their own markets, including their own sensitive industrial sectors. As a result, the liberalisation of FDI can provoke controversial issues with regard to several industrial sectors, especially those of nuclear energy, aircraft, infrastructure, military equipment, and so on.

There are two articles in the TPP which refer to the liberalisation of FDI, that is, Article 9.4 (National Treatment or NT) and Article 9.5 (Most-Favoured-Nation or MFN treatment).[4] Article 9.4 provides the following.

Article 9.4: National Treatment

1. Each Party shall accord to investors of another Party treatment no less favourable than that it accords, in like circumstances, to its own investors with respect to the *establishment*, *acquisition*, expansion, management, conduct, operation, and sale or other disposition of investments in its territory.
2. Each Party shall accord to covered investments treatment no less favourable than that it accords, in like circumstances, to investments in its territory of its own investors with respect to the *establishment*, *acquisition*, expansion, management, conduct, operation, and sale or other disposition of investments. (emphasis added)

The important terms here are 'establishment' and 'acquisition'. These terms mean that the host States have to treat the foreign investors/investments and domestic investors/investments equally, right from the moment of starting the investment (i.e. at the 'establishment' and 'acquisition' phase).[5] Consequently, the host States are prohibited from excluding foreign investors/investments from their own markets.[6]

[4]Article 9.5 stipulates the MFN treatment, and it also uses the terms 'establishment' and 'acquisition' for this purpose. This means that the MFN treatment must be applied right from the pre-establishment phase of foreign investment.

[5]Generally, there are two phases of investment: *pre-establishment* phase and *post-establishment* phase. In other words, if the NT obligation applies to the pre-establishment phase (i.e. pre-investment national treatment), this is regarded as liberalisation of FDI.

[6]Two examples were mentioned as consequences of liberalisation of investment. First, in Viet Nam, the small retailer sector was to be opened to foreign investors, and Viet Nam will be obliged to abolish its domestic regulations such as the ENT (Economic Needs Test) in this context. For more information on this point, see 'Annex I - Viet Nam' which touches upon the 'Distribution services' sector and clarifies that 'five years after the date of entry into force of this Agreement for Viet Nam, the ENT shall be removed and this entry shall no longer have effect'. Second, in Malaysia, the small retailer sector will be opened to foreign investors.

For example, if State A wants to join the TPP, it has to abolish or amend its domestic law which prohibits the acquisition of shares of a company in the nuclear energy industry. It is thus clear that the liberalisation of investment has the huge impact of opening the domestic market to foreign investors. At the same time, however, this may create a dangerous situation for the host States.

It should be noted that, on the one hand, the liberalisation of investment has a huge (detrimental) impact on the domestic market, as we saw above. Against this trend, there are two options for the contracting parties to be exempted from the application of Articles 9.4 and 9.5. One is the general exception clause, and the other is the NCM clause.

9.3.2 Exception Clause of the TPP

Like any other FTA, the TPP contains an important chapter of exception, that is, Chapter 29 'Exceptions and general provision'. In particular, Article 29.2 (Security Exceptions) provides the following.

Nothing in this Agreement shall be construed to:

(a) require a Party to furnish or allow access to any information the disclosure of which it determines to be contrary to its essential security interests, or
(b) preclude a Party from applying measures that it considers necessary for the fulfilment of its obligations with respect to *the maintenance or restoration of international peace or security*, or *the protection of its own essential security interests*. (emphasis added)

First, according to paragraph (b), a contracting Party is allowed to take measures which it considers necessary not only for 'international peace or security', but also for the 'protection of its own essential security interests'. The former aims at, for example, the compliance of the obligation imposed by the Resolutions of the United Nations Security Council. The latter, on the other hand, can extend to the individual interest of contracting parties for the protection of their own 'essential security'. As a consequence, if there are 'essential security interests', any contracting party can be exempted from applying the TPP articles, including the investment chapter.

Second, paragraph (b) transplants Article 21 of GATT (security exceptions) and Article 14 bis of the General Agreement on Trade in Services (GATS) (security exceptions) into the TPP, but it does not contain any explanation of concrete measures included in that paragraph. Consequently, it is reasonable to think that this paragraph extends to measures indicated in Article 21 (b) of GATT and Article 14 bis (b) of GATS, but is not limited to these. In any case, determining the extent of 'essential security interests' in actual cases is problematic.

9.3.3 Non-conforming Measures Under the TPP

The second exception is stipulated in the provision of non-conforming measures, which admits exceptions to several fundamental clauses such as the NT (Article 9.4) and MFN (Article 9.5) clauses. Article 9.12 of the TPP provides the following.

Article 9.12: Non-Conforming Measures

1. Article 9.4 (National Treatment), Article 9.5 (Most-Favoured-Nation Treatment), Article 9.10 (Performance Requirements), and Article 9.11 (Senior Management and Boards of Directors) shall not apply to:

   (a) any existing non-conforming measure that is maintained by a Party at:

      (i) the central level of government, as set out by that Party in its Schedule to Annex I,
      (ii) a regional level of government, as set out by that Party in its Schedule to Annex I, or
      (iii) a local level of government;

   (b) the continuation or prompt renewal of any non-conforming measure referred to in subparagraph (a); or
   (c) an amendment to any non-conforming measure referred to in subparagraph (a), to the extent that the amendment does not decrease the conformity of the measure, as it existed immediately before the amendment, with Article 9.4 (National Treatment), Article 9.5 (Most-Favoured-Nation Treatment), Article 9.10 (Performance Requirements), or Article 9.11 (Senior Management and Boards of Directors).

2. Article 9.4, Article 9.5, Article 9.10, and Article 9.11 shall not apply to any measure that a Party adopts or maintains with respect to sectors, subsectors, or activities, as set out by that Party in its Schedule to Annex II.

This clause has the following characteristics. *First*, unlike the general exception clause (Article 29.2), the NCM clause targets the exemption of contracting countries from particular obligations such as NT (Art 9.4), MFN (Art 9.5), Performance Requirement (Art 9.10), and Senior Management and Boards of Directors (Art 9.11). Thus, it is clear that the NCM clause aims to be an exception to the liberalisation of investment. While the targeted obligations are limited to the above four, there is no need to explain the reason for listing the particular measures in the Annexes. On this point, the NCM clause has a different function from that of the general exception clause (Article 29.2). The latter requires the existence of particular reasons for exceptions, such as 'security interests'. However, in the case of the NCM clause, a contracting party can list any sector in the Annexes without providing a reason for choosing it. *Second*, according to the NCM clause, particular industrial sectors designated in the Annexes can be exempted from the application of the above obligations. As we see below, each contracting party attaches Annexes to the main text of the TPP. To put it simply, the NCM clause is equivalent to the reservation under the Vienna Convention on the Law of Treaties.[7] As a result of Article 9.12 and the attached Annex in accordance with it, the contracting parties can maintain their measures for excluding foreign investors/investments from some sectors; that is, it is possible for them to protect their sensitive industrial sectors.

There are four categories of regulation in the non-conforming measures, depending on the actors (central level, regional level, or local level), and in each case Annex I and Annex II are applied differently. It is thus necessary to check each Annex in order to conclude whether a particular measure is exempted from the relevant articles.

Non-conforming measures	Actors	Annex	Article
Existing measures	The central level of government	Annex I	9.12.1(a)(i)/9.12.1 (b)
	Regional level of government	Annex I	9.12.1(a)(ii)/9.12.1 (b)
	Local level of government	No Annex	9.12.1(a)(iii)/9.12.1 (b)
Any measure	Party	Annex II	9.12.2

We refer to the Annexes attached by Japan as an example. Japan made two Annexes, '**Annex I-JAPAN**' and '**Annex II-JAPAN**' which mention 56 sectors and 14 sectors respectively. These sectors are Japan's sensitive industrial sectors. For example, the 'Aerospace Industry', 'Arms and Explosives Industry', and 'Information and Communications Industry' are listed.

Among them, Social Security Services, especially the Japan Post Insurance Co. Ltd. (the so-called 'Kanpo-Seimei-Hoken') was the most controversial sector for Japan during the TPP negotiation. This was because it is the biggest insurance company in the world, with a total property amounting to USD 959 billion. Thus, Japan clarifies its exemption from national treatment (see No. 11 in '**Annex II-JAPAN**').[8]

No. 56 of **Annex I-Japan** is also of relevance, as it touches upon the aerospace industry sector (in particular, the 'Aircraft Manufacturing and Repairing Industry' sub-sector). The NT clause is exempted (Articles 9.4 and 10.3), and the non-conforming measures are Articles 27 and 30 of the Foreign Exchange and Foreign Trade Law (Law No. 228 of 1949), Articles 3 and 5 of the Cabinet Order on Foreign Direct Investment (Cabinet Order No. 261 of 1980), and Article 2

[7]See Articles 19 to 23 of the Vienna Convention on the Law of Treaties.

[8]The exempted sector is 'Public Law Enforcement and Correctional Services and Social Services', and the description is as follows: 'Japan reserves the right to adopt or maintain any measure relating to investments or the supply of services in public law enforcement and correctional services, and in social services established or maintained for a public purpose: income security or insurance, social security or insurance, social welfare, public training, health, child care, and public housing'.

through 5 of the Aircraft Manufacturing Industry Law (Law No. 237 of 1952). Furthermore, it is explained that

1. The prior notification requirement and screening procedures under the Foreign Exchange and Foreign Trade Law apply to foreign investors who intended to make investments in the aircraft industry in Japan.
2. The screening is conducted from the viewpoint of whether the investment is likely to cause a situation in which *national security* is impaired, the maintenance of *public order* is disturbed, or the protection of *public safety* is hindered.
3. The investors may be required to alter the content of the investment or discontinue the investment process, depending on the screening result. (emphasis added)

Thus, it is here clear that the pre-establishment NT obligation is not imposed on the Japanese measures restricting inward FDI as far as the same apply to the aircraft manufacturing sector, and consequently, Japan can maintain its law and regulation which excludes inward FDI in this sector.

Other examples of sectors listed in Japan's Annexes include the following. **Annex I-Japan** lists Heat Supply (No. 10), Information Communication [Sub-sector: Telecommunications (No. 11)], and Oil Industry (No. 20). **Annex II-Japan** lists Aerospace Industry (No. 4), Arms and Explosives Industry (No. 5), Information and Communications (No. 6), Energy [Sub-sector: Nuclear Energy Industry (No. 8)], Security Guard Services (No. 12), and Transport [Sub-sector: Air Transport (No. 13)]. It is possible to understand that these listed sectors can be regarded as sensitive sectors for Japan which is willing to maintain the protective measures and to exclude inward FDI in these sectors. As a consequence, in the case of the TPP with regard to these sectors, Japan's domestic law and regulations still apply, as we see below.

As stated previously, the TPP allows contracting parties to be exempted from the liberalisation of FDI by admitting the non-conforming measures. This manner of exemption will become increasingly important and complex. This is because, *first*, as liberalisation is enhanced and expanded in the TPP, additional industrial sectors will be subject to FDI, thus provoking concerns from the parties. *Second*, the non-conforming measures are necessary since the TPP covers twelve different States; in other words, the States' development levels vary, and thus, each country has different sensitive sectors.

9.4 Balance Between Investment and Security in Domestic Law

There are many regulations pertaining to inward FDI with regard to security interests on the domestic level as well. The most famous one is the Exon-Florio Amendment of the U.S.A. In this section, we examine the Japanese Act which functions to exclude FDI on the basis of security interests.

9.4.1 Japan's Foreign Exchange and Foreign Trade Act

In 1949, Japan enacted the Foreign Exchange and Foreign Trade Act,[9] which regulates inward direct investment (Chap. 5), as well as payments (Chap. 3), capital transactions (Chap. 4), and foreign trade (Chap. 6). With regard to foreign investment, the Act regulates outward investment (Article 23) and inward investment (Articles 26 and 27). There are several important articles with regard to inward FDI.

First, Article 26(2) defines 'inward direct investment' as follows:

(i) Acquisition of the shares or equity of a corporation […],
(ii) […],
(iii) Acquisition of the shares of a Listed Corporation, etc. (limited to cases where the ratio of the number of shares of the Listed Corporation, etc. […] is not less than the ratio specified by Cabinet Order which is not less than 10%).

Second, with regard to the risk of inward FDI damaging security interests, the Act adopts the prior notification mechanism. Article 27(1) provides for this purpose, as seen below.

> When a foreign investor intends to make an inward direct investment […] specified by the Cabinet Order as being likely to fall under inward direct investment, which requires examination pursuant to paragraph 3, *he/she shall notify in advance*, pursuant to the provisions of Cabinet Order, the Minister of Finance and the minister having jurisdiction over the business of the business purpose, amount, time of making the investment and other matters specified by Cabinet Order in regard to the inward direct investment. (emphasis added)

It should be noted that prior notification is required by the Act, contrary to the post-report regime adopted in the Exon-Florio Amendment in the U.S.A.

Third, with regard to the notification, prior to the actual inward FDI, the Government takes into consideration the following factors, according to Article 27 (3)(i).

(a) National security is impaired, the maintenance of public order is disturbed, or the protection of public safety is hindered.
(b) Significant adverse effect is brought to the smooth management of the Japanese economy.

[9] Act No. 228 of 1 December 1949.

9.4.2 Implementation of the Act: The J-Power Case

The Act contains two steps for implementation, namely, a recommendation [Article 27(5)][10] and an order [Article 27(10)],[11] by which the Minister of Finance discourages and refuses inward FDI. Thus far, the Act has been implemented in one concrete case only, in accordance with Article 27: the J-Power case (2008).

In this case, the Children's Investment Fund (TCI), a U.K.-based hedge fund, was seeking to raise its stake in the J-Power Electric Power Development Co., from 9.9 to 20%. In order to achieve this goal, the TCI requested, in accordance with the requirement under the Foreign Trade Act, the approval of the Japanese Government, before acquiring more than 10 percent of J-Power's shares. On 16 April 2008, the Government, in the form of the above-mentioned recommendation, rejected this request, citing a potential threat to public policy under Article 27 of the Act. This recommendation was based on the Opinion rendered by the Council on Customs, Tariff, Foreign Exchange and other Transactions on 15 April 2008.[12]

According to the Opinion, the public order should not be hampered by FDI. The electricity industry, which constitutes basic infrastructure, is one of areas covered by FDI regulations under the OECD Code, and the long-term and stable supply of electricity has been maintained by this treatment. The J-Power Co. plans to establish the Oma nuclear power plant, which is important for the national nuclear and nuclear fuel cycle policy. It cannot be denied that if the TCI acquired additional shares of J-Power, its actions could pose the risk of bearing unexpected influence on the implementation of the above mentioned policy. Based on this Opinion, the Japanese Government applied Article 27 of the Act and recommended the cessation of holding shares (16 April 2008). Since the TCI neglected this recommendation, the Japanese Government *ordered* the cessation of investment, in accordance with Article 27(10) on 13 May 2008. The TCI finally abandoned the FDI in this case.

The J-Power case was the first to which Article 27 of the Foreign Trade Act (the recommendation and order procedure) was applied. On the one hand, as is shown in this case, the restriction of inward FDI in the electricity industry is universally

[10]Article 27(5) provides that, 'the Minister of Finance [...] may *recommend* a person who has given notification of the inward direct investment to change the content pertaining to the inward direct investment or discontinue the inward direct investment pursuant to the provisions of Cabinet Order after hearing opinions of the Council on Customs, Tariff, Foreign Exchange and other Transactions'. (emphasis added).

[11]Article 27(10) provides that, 'Where a person [...] has not given a notice pursuant to the provision of paragraph 7 or has given a notice of refusal of the recommendation, the Minister of Finance and the minister [...] may *order* the person to change the content pertaining to the inward direct investment or to discontinue the inward direct investment'. (emphasis added).

[12]The Opinion of 15 April 2008 was made public (in Japanese) and is available at [https://www.mof.go.jp/about_mof/councils/customs_foreign_exchange/sub-foreign_exchange/report/gaishibukaiiken.pdf].

admitted (the OECD Code of 1960). On the other hand, it can be said that the criteria of 'public order' and 'risk', both applied in this case, are too vague and ambiguous to be applied to other situations.

9.5 Conclusions

It is necessary to consider the conflict between investment and security, especially with the increase in FDI in global terms.

First, export controls must cover not only trade relations, but also investment relations, because the latter are deeply related to the security concerns of the host State. If a foreign investor were to own more than half the share of a company belonging to a military industry, for example, the host State's security interests would be at high risk; this is why there is considerable control over investment under international law and domestic law.

Second, the liberalisation of investment requires many countries to open their markets to foreign investors and to invite the latter into their markets. As a result, the liberalisation of investment increases the risk of conflict between investment and security.

Third, in order to avoid or settle the above conflict, international law has established two mechanisms. One is the general exception clause, which allows the contracting parties to be exempted from the application of a treaty if security interests are at stake. The second is the non-conforming measures clause which can function as a reservation and is applicable to particular industrial sectors. Thus, it is necessary to be aware of these two mechanisms simultaneously.

Fourth, there is evidence of collaboration between international law and domestic law. In the case of Japan, the Foreign Exchange and Foreign Trade Act has been applied to exclude inward FDI in some cases. However, this kind of domestic law is not in conformity with the clause promoting liberalisation of investment (i.e. the pre-NT clause). This is why the NCM clause is needed to maintain the domestic law which controls inward FDI. In other words, there is collaboration between international law (the NCM clause) and domestic law (the Foreign Trade Act) in the field of investment control.

Chapter 10
Responsive Action or Emerging Strategy? Japan's Revision of Its Arms Transfer Policy

Tomoaki Ishigaki

Abstract This article examines the recent revision of Japan's arms export policy in the broader context of international rule-making under the Arms Trade Treaty, Japan's increased involvement in peacekeeping and regional security affairs as well as the challenge faced by its domestic defense industry. The 2014 revision of the Three Principles on Transfer of Defense Equipment and Technology was based on various practical reasons. The first was the need to adapt the logistical foundation of the Japanese defense industry. More importantly, the change was made possible because of the increase in public support for Japan to engage in international activities in UN peacekeeping and other security-related programs, the expertise gained through such activities as well as the public awareness of the rapidly shifting security environment in the region. Japan may not drastically increase its arms exports and will continue to comply with the various international disarmament instruments it has supported.

Keywords Japan · Asia · Arms trade treaty · Export control · UN peacekeeping operations

10.1 Introduction

Throughout the post-World War II era, Japan has been recognized as a global economic power, but not a military power due to its constitutional restriction on waging war and its limited arms exports. Japan has advanced its disarmament agenda at various multilateral fora including the United Nations (UN), on both

Counsellor, Cabinet Legislation Bureau, INGEER Conference Government of Japan at the time of the first in November 2015. He currently serves as the Director of Climate Change Division at the Ministry of Foreign Affairs of Japan. The views expressed in this article are personal and do not necessarily reflect the views of the government.

T. Ishigaki (✉)
Climate Change Division, Ministry of Foreign Affairs of Japan, Tokyo, Japan
e-mail: tomoaki.ishigaki@mofa.go.jp

D. Tamada and P. Achilleas (eds.), *Theory and Practice of Export Control*,
Kobe University Social Science Research Series,
DOI 10.1007/978-981-10-5960-5_10

nuclear and conventional weapons; it has also promoted a number of nonproliferation initiatives. Most recently, as one of the original cosponsors, Japan became one of the earliest members of the Arms Trade Treaty (ATT). Given such a track record, it could come as a surprise to see Japan's recent revision of its arms export policy, increasing the possibility that it would export defense equipment and technologies to other countries aside from its ally the United States.

The changing security environment in East Asia in recent years can be cited as a key reason for Japan's shift to a more robust security policy. The Japanese government revised its interpretation of Japan's right under its constitution to exercise its right of collective defense—although it is still limited—and introduced domestic legislation that mandates the Self-Defense Forces (SDF) to take more active measures. The recent change in the arms export policy can be seen as a part of this general shift. Some even argue that this significant shift in Japan's policy is a departure from its traditional policy on multilateral disarmament and nonproliferation. As yet, however, few studies have been made, owing to the newness of the subject matter.[1]

Japan's change in its arms transfer policy should be seen not only as a part of the recently introduced domestic security legislations, but also from a broader perspective. This article takes the position that the revision of the policy is the culmination of various security-related policies ranging from UN peacekeeping operations to disaster relief and global rulemaking, as well as the acquisition policy of defense technology. To better understand the background of this change, this article also outlines the incremental changes made in the Three Principles on Arms Exports over the past forty years. The change in Japan's arms transfer policy was made possible by the country's increased involvement in security affairs, both in the region and around the world. Japan may not drastically increase its arms exports and will continue to comply with the various international disarmament instruments it has supported. How Japan preserves its image as a strong advocate of multilateral rules on export control depends on the way it applies those rules.

10.2 Japan's Profile on Disarmament and Nonproliferation[2]

Japan has been a consistent supporter of multilateral frameworks on arms control and nonproliferation since it rejoined international society in the early 1950s. Japan supported the Treaty on the Non-Proliferation of Nuclear Weapons (NPT) and

[1]A preliminary commentary on this subject can be found at Heigo Sato, "From the 'Three Principles of Arms Exports' to the 'Three Principles of Defense Equipment Transfer,'" AJISS-Commentary No. 197 (Japan Institute of International Affairs 2014), available at https://www.2.jiia.or.jp/en_commentary/201405/14-1.html.

[2]An overview of Japan's recent policy on disarmament and nonproliferation can be found in *Diplomatic Bluebook 2015*, available at http://www.mofa.go.jp/policy/other/bluebook/2015/html/chapter3/c030104.html.

accepted inspections by the International Atomic Energy Agency from early years. Japan is one of the few countries that submit almost all the reports required by various UN sanctions committees, informing them of the domestic legislation and measures taken to prevent the proliferation of materials and technologies related to weapons of mass destruction. Japan was instrumental in establishing a number of agreements and mechanisms at the UN, such as the Arms Trade Treaty (ATT),[3] UN Programme of Action on Small Arms and Light Weapons (POA), and UN Registry on Conventional Arms. Japan also attaches great importance to legally nonbinding yet critically important frameworks such as the Missile Technology Control Regime, Proliferation Security Initiative,[4] Wassenaar Arrangement, and Australia Group, incorporating the standards adopted by these frameworks into its export regulations.

On the domestic front, Japan has developed a framework for a public-private partnership to address export control issues. The collaboration between the government and the Center for Information on Security Trade Controls (CISTEC),[5] an industry-led association, has promoted a voluntary compliance mechanism on export control. The government has also worked with nongovernmental organizations to promote disarmament and nonproliferation, especially through awareness building and public education.[6] Furthermore, Japan for nearly forty years, since 1967, maintained its restrictive policy on arms exports known as the Three Principles on Arms Exports.[7] Under these principles, the export of Japanese defense equipment and technology was allowed only in very limited cases, such as exports to its ally the United States, and to assist some peacekeeping and peacebuilding efforts. All these activities were seen as testaments to Japan's strong commitment on export control issues.

Against this backdrop, on April 1, 2014, the government revised the Three Principles on Arms Exports, recasting them as the Three Principles on Transfer of

---

[3]Japan's efforts to create the ATT can be found at "The Adoption of the Arms Trade Treaty Overview and Assessment (Overview and Assessment)" on the Ministry of Foreign Affairs (MOFA) website, http://www.mofa.go.jp/policy/page3e_000005.html.

[4]Japan's involvement in various PSI exercises can be found at "The Proliferation Security Initiative," MOFA, *supra* note 4, http://www.mofa.go.jp/policy/un/disarmament/arms/psi/psi.html.

[5]An overview of CISTEC can be found on its website at http://www.cistec.or.jp/english/about/index.html.

[6]An overview of the cooperation between the Japanese government and civil society on disarmament education can be found in Tomoaki Ishigaki, "Collaboration between Governments and civil society on disarmament and non-proliferation education," in *The Importance of Civil Society in United Nations and Intergovernmental Processes: Views from Four Delegates to the United Nations* 13–22 (United Nations Office for Disarmament Affairs 2015), available at http://www.un.org/disarmament/publications/civilsociety/en/civil-society-2014.pdf.

[7]The full text of the Three Principles on Arms Exports can be found at "Japan's Policies on the Control of Arms Exports," MOFA, *supra* note 4, http://www.mofa.go.jp/policy/un/disarmament/policy/.

Defense Equipment and Technology. While some welcomed this initiative as Japan's expressed commitment to be more active in global security affairs, criticism for the revision also exists. Critics pointed out that Japan would become another arms exporter and would possibly fuel conflicts.[8] Concerns were increased because this new policy was announced very shortly after February 25, 2014, when the government submitted the ATT for approval by Japan's parliament, the Diet.[9]

10.3 Three Principles in Political and Historical Context

To understand the reason behind the recent change in Japan's policy on arms transfer, one must first know the political, historical, and economic context behind the original Three Principles on Arms Exports introduced in 1967.[10] In the original formulation of the principles, the government prohibited the export of arms to three areas: (1) communist countries, (2) countries under UN arms embargo, and (3) countries parties to international armed conflict. There was no restriction on exporting arms to countries other than these three categories. In 1976, Prime Minister Takeo Miki stated that Japan would refrain from exporting arms even to countries not covered by those three categories. In short, the guideline announced that Japan basically would not export arms to *any* countries. The Three Principles as reformulated by Prime Minister Miki went through a slight modification in 1983. Due to the need to engage in joint research and development of defense equipment and technology with the United States, the Japanese government made it possible to have case-by-case exemptions from the Three Principles for such bilateral programs. Since then, twenty-one cases of exemptions have been granted[11] for the bilateral defense cooperation with the United States and provision of military equipment for peacekeeping operations.

The restrictive policy was made possible and survived for nearly four decades for various political and economic reasons. First, there was a strong need for Japan to associate itself with western democracies during the Cold War and be a strong supporter of the export control regime including the Coordinating Committee for Multilateral Export Controls (CoCom). This was during the time when the Japanese economy and trade were booming and the US and European governments criticized Japan for its aggressive exports. The Toshiba Machinery case[12] made many

[8]See, for example, an editorial in *Asahi Shimbun* (April 3, 2014), available at http://ajw.asahi.com/article/views/editorial/AJ201404030031.

[9]Cautious words of welcome were made by civil society members toward Japan's ratification of the ATT. An example can be found at http://controlarms.org/en/news/japan-ratifies-arms-trade-treaty-entry-into-force-one-step-closer/.

[10]More details can be found at MOFA, *supra* note 8.

[11]Source: Fact sheet of the Cabinet Secretariat, which is available (only in Japanese) at http://www.cas.go.jp/jp/gaiyou/jimu/pdf/bouei5.pdf (at 9 of the fact sheet).

[12]Wrubel (1989).

Japanese manufacturers realize the critical importance of compliance, paving the way for the establishment of the research and cooperative association, CISTEC.[13] Japan had to prove itself as a rule-abiding partner.

Second, there was a strong domestic political reason for maintaining such restraint. During the conservative government under the Liberal Democratic Party, the government and its policies were often regarded in some people's eyes as too hawkish and pro-American. Promotion of a pacifist and nonmilitary agenda gained bipartisan support and was considered effective in gaining a broader political base.

Third, on the economic and technological front, there were no strong business interests that advocated arms export. The Japanese defense industry was still a beneficiary of the technology transfer from the United States. The US industry and government also increased their interest in technology transfer from Japan, especially after 1980s when Japanese technology became competitive. The ad hoc exemptions from the Three Principles were considered by the Japanese government and industry to ensure bilateral defense cooperation. Furthermore, the Self-Defense Forces were the sole customer for the Japanese defense industry, and until the 1980s the industry was able to maintain business as the defense budget gradually grew. For these reasons, there was not a strong rationale in Japan throughout the Cold War to support the export of its arms overseas.

10.4 Undercurrent for Changing the Three Principles

Since the end of the Cold War in the early 1990s, Japan has become more active in undertaking various responsibilities on global security issues, gaining more experience through development assistance, security cooperation, and global rulemaking. In addition, the change in technology also required Japan to reconsider its acquisition and development policy. The culmination of these developments served as a groundwork for preparing the Japanese government, business, and general public for revision of the Three Principles. It is therefore insufficient to categorize Japan's policy shift on arms transfer simply as a part of recent change in Japan's defense policy that allowed the SDF to take measures to exercise the right of collective self-defense.[14]

---

[13] CISTEC was founded in 1989, shortly after the Toshiba Machinery case. See http://www.cistec.or.jp/english/about/introE2.html#annaie1 for more details. The unique nature of CISTEC's activities is explained in Hideaki Shiroyama, *Japan's Export Control Becoming More Globalized* (越境する日本の安全保障貿易管理) 59–72 (Public Policy Studies Association (公共政策研究) 2007), available (only in Japanese) at http://www.ppsa.jp/pdf/93.pdf.

[14] As Sato points out, unlike the recent passage of security legislation where ruling and opposition parties differed in their views, the revision of the arms transfer policy had bipartisan support. The first change in the most recent series of revisions was made when the Democratic Party of Japan was in power in 2011. See *supra* note 2.

10.4.1 Synergy Between Security and Development

First, Japan's active involvement on developmental issues made it more practical to use its expertise on controlling arms. Based on its forty-year experience with foreign aid, Japan came to believe that the unregulated flow of arms has often resulted in prolonging conflicts, especially in African and Asian states. Calling conventional weapons "de facto weapons of mass destruction," Japan established a Small Arms Fund at the UN in 2000[15] and provided various forms of assistance to collect and destroy surplus arms, train former soldiers, and bring them back to the community. These activities, which are often called "disarmament, demobilization, and reintegration" (DDR) took place in various post-conflict zones, and Japan was active in many of these countries.[16] The Japanese government and industry also took part in research and development programs for demining, using Japanese technological capabilities.[17] There was wide public support for these programs because they combined both developmental and humanitarian considerations for post-conflict communities. In these activities, the government approved exceptions to the Three Principles to provide demining machinery, bulletproof vests, and helmets, which were categorized as weapons under the Japanese laws.[18]

10.4.2 Active Involvement in Security Assistance

Second, Japan became active not only on developmental issues, but also on regional security issues. One of the groundbreaking cases was the provision of patrol boats to the Indonesian Coast Guard in 2006.[19] This was created as a bilateral grant aid

---

[15]The Small Arms Fund was announced at the G8 Foreign Ministers meeting in Miyazaki in April 2000 and was funded in the amount of $2 million. See more details in *Diplomatic Bluebook 2001*, available at http://www.mofa.go.jp/policy/other/bluebook/2001/chap2-1-b.html.

[16]For the detailed list of Japan's activities in DDR, regional assistance, and awareness-raising programs in relation to small arms and light weapons, see Japan's National Report regarding the implementation of the Programme of Action, especially pp. 16–30, which can be found at http://www.poa-iss.org/CASACountryProfile/PoANationalReports/2012@98@PoA-ITI-Japan-2012.pdf.

[17]For the details of research and development programs for demining technologies, see the pamphlet of the MOFA, "Toward a World Without Mines," available at http://www.mofa.go.jp/policy/landmine/pamph0411.pdf. Examples of collaboration between civil society and private companies can also be found in *Diplomatic Bluebook 2013*, in an article featuring the role of companies such as Komatsu, Sumitomo, and Toyota Tsusho. This source is available at http://www.mofa.go.jp/policy/oda/white/2013/html/column/column12.html.

[18]The list of exemptions can be found in the Cabinet Secretariat information, *supra* note 12 (available only in Japanese).

[19]See *Japan's Official Development Assistance White Paper 2006*, available at http://www.mofa.go.jp/policy/oda/white/2006/ODA2006/html/honpen/hp202040400.htm.

project with an objective of enhancing Indonesia's antipiracy capabilities. There was a clear recognition among government officials of the need to incorporate security considerations in the developmental needs of the country to be assisted.[20] In this case, too, the exemption from the Three Principles was sought and granted. The patrol boats did not have weapons mounted (and they were to be furnished by the Indonesian side), but because of the specification of the vessel, it was categorized as arms and needed to be exempted from the Three Principles.

Another case around the same period was the provision of patrol cars, police buses, and motorbikes to Iraqi police forces, and ambulances and fire engines to Iraqi municipalities, between 2004 and 2011.[21] Because Japan's traditional aid policy was cautious in assisting security and law enforcement bodies, this was clearly a policy-driven assistance in combination with the political decision to send Self-Defense Forces to Iraq. These vehicles were deployed in many cases of terrorist attacks, and they played a critical role in maintaining public order in Iraqi cities and communities during difficult times.

The third example is the provision of used equipment of the SDF engineering corps, sent to post-conflict and disaster-stricken areas such as East Timor and Haiti. The SDF equipment such as bulldozers and excavators (power shovels) was categorized as weapons because they have mounts for equipping firearms, and the exemption was needed for them to be donated to the local entities.[22]

These examples show that Japan's involvement in promoting peace and stability as well as economic and social development in post-conflict and disaster areas had a growing security dimension. Although Japan's first participation in UN peacekeeping activities in 1992 (deployment SDF to Cambodia) was met with much criticism from the public at beginning, its participation has now gained a majority of public support.[23] After more than twenty years of the successful deployment of SDF missions to Cambodia, Mozambique, Rwanda, Honduras, East Timor, the

[20]The Japanese government introduced a new assistance program, the Grant Aid for Cooperation on Counter-Terrorism and Security Enhancement in 2006 and provided various assistance mainly to Asian countries. The details can be found at http://www.mofa.go.jp/policy/terrorism/intl_coop.html.

[21]For examples, see *Japan's Official Development Assistance White Paper 2007*, available at http://www.mofa.go.jp/policy/oda/white/2007/ODA2007/html/honpen/hp202020402.htm. Also, the fact sheet on Japan's assistance toward Iraq (as of August 2009) is available at http://www.mofa.go.jp/region/middle_e/iraq/issue2003/assistance/assist0610.pdf.

[22]The provision of bulldozers by the SDF in Haiti is briefly referred to in Hikaru Yamashita, *Peacekeeping Trends and National Responses: A Japanese Perspective* (paper presented at the NIDS International Symposium on Security Affairs 2014), available at http://www.nids.go.jp/english/event/symposium/pdf/2014/E-08.pdf. The description of the SDF's activities in Haiti can be found at http://www.mod.go.jp/e/jdf/no17/current.html.

[23]According to the survey conducted in October 2014, approximately 80% of the public supported Japan's participation in UN Peacekeeping Operations. See Sect. 2 (Public Opinion) of "Japan's Contributions Based on the International Peace Cooperation Act," MOFA, *supra* note 4, http://www.mofa.go.jp/fp/ipc/page22e_000684.html.

Golan Heights, Djibouti, Iraq, Haiti, Indonesia, Nepal, the Philippines, and South Sudan, there is a growing positive image for the use of Japan's military capabilities, especially through UN peacekeeping operations, disaster relief, and overseas development assistance.[24] Accordingly, Japan's assistance in security areas has become less politically controversial over the years.

10.4.3 Changing Security Environment and Need for Transparency

Third, apart from Japan's increased involvement in global security and developmental agenda, geopolitical changes forced Japan to adapt to newly emerging circumstances. On the international front, the increase in regional military expenditure as well as political tensions compelled Japan to be even more active in multilateral rulemaking. Domestically, Japan faced serious challenges in maintaining its production platform for defense equipment.

Global arms transfer has been on the rise since the 2000s with a brief exception during the financial crisis in 2008. The strong drive of such expansion is led by two regions, the Middle East and Asia. Asia did not have any major armed conflicts after the Vietnam War, the civil war in Cambodia, and the struggle for independence in East Timor in 2002. Nevertheless, the military expenditure in the region has been constantly on the rise. It has been accelerated by China's military modernization, followed by other countries such as India and the Southeast Asian states. The trend is evident in the statistics, where the global share of arms import in Asia-Oceania is the highest and has increased from 40 percent to 48 percent in the two periods of 2005–2009 and 2010–2014.[25] Furthermore, of the ten largest importers of major weapons in 2010–2014, India, China, Pakistan, Australia, South Korea, and Singapore are placed first, third, fifth, sixth, ninth, and tenth.

Needless to mention, the recent tension over territorial disputes on the South China Sea has contributed to a growing concern on where and how arms are being transferred. There is also continuous military provocation made by North Korea with its nuclear tests, missile launches, and other proliferation activities. All these developments have made Japan more vigilant and active in articulating global rules on arms transfers that enhance transparency and hold states more accountable for their behavior. This was one of the main reasons why Japan was active in promoting rulemaking on global arms transfers through the Arms Trade Treaty. The Japanese delegation stressed the need to include the rules and provisions for

[24]A list of deployments of Japan's SDF under the International Peace Cooperation Act is given in "Japan's Contributions Based on the International Peace Cooperation Act," MOFA, *supra* note 4, http://www.mofa.go.jp/fp/ipc/page22e_000684.html.

[25]See Wezeman and Wezeman (2014).

mandatory reporting, publication of national reports, and transfer records, as well as capacity building for developing countries in need of implementation of export control measures.[26]

10.4.4 Acquisition and Joint Development Program

Fourth, the logistical challenge regarding the acquisition of high-end military equipment also caused a practical need for the government to revisit its Three Principles. One of the major reasons Japanese companies could not participate in the joint development of arms was the strict limitation on the third-party use of the equipment and technology transferred from Japan to other countries. The existing guidelines became too restrictive to respond to the recent trend of involving multiple partners in the joint development programs, such as the JSF/F-35 program.

In addition, with the continuous drop in Japan's military budget, the Japanese defense industry has been facing serious challenges in maintaining its domestic production base.[27] With the globalized supply chain and worldwide procurement of parts and components from manufacturers, many international defense industries started creating joint projects to share the financial burden and also to reduce production costs of each unit. In the meantime, the restriction of third-party use and technology transfers became a major obstacle for Japanese firms as they could not participate in these projects or compete against other international manufacturers to produce high-quality and price-competitive defense equipment. Aggravated by the dwindling demands in the domestic defense market, it is reported that of the 1500 defense-related companies in Japan (including the suppliers of rations and other basic supplies), more than 100 companies have withdrawn from the market over the past ten years.[28]

Faced with such a growing need to revisit the Three Principles, the liberal-leaning government led by the Democratic Party of Japan revised the policy in 2013, paving the way for joint development and provision of defense equipment for UN peacekeeping operations and other international cooperation activities. However, the change did not sufficiently address the issue of Japan's participation in the international logistical support system (especially for providing parts and

---

[26]Regarding Japan's negotiating history at the ATT, see Tomoaki Ishigaki (2014), especially 404–409 on the negotiations concerning the transparency clause.

[27]A similar point was made by Sato. See Heigo Sato, *Japan's Arms Export and Defense Production Policy* 5 (Center for Strategic & International Studies 2015), http://csis.org/files/publication/150331_Sato_JapanArmsExport.pdf.

[28]Report from the Research Group on Defense Production and Technology Platform, June 2012, especially 19, available (only in Japanese) at http://www.mod.go.jp/j/approach/agenda/meeting/seisan/houkoku/finalreport.html. Established in November 2010, the Research Group deliberated for eighteen months to submit a proposal to the Ministry of Defense regarding a strategy to maintain and foster a defense production and technology platform.

components) and the provision of test samples for feasibility studies of joint research and development.

10.5 The New Three Principles

10.5.1 Overview

The government decided on April 1, 2014, to introduce the Three Principles on Transfer of Defense Equipment and Technology.[29] The three-page policy paper describes under what circumstances the government permits or denies the transfer of defense equipment and technology and how the transfer would be conducted. Following is a summary of the ideas presented in the new Three Principles.

- There will remain a ban on export of arms that constitute violations of international obligations or UN Security Council Resolutions, as well as on provision of arms to a country that is party to a conflict.
- Transfers will be limited to cases where appropriate control is ensured. The government will require the recipient government to gain Japan's prior consent regarding the transfer to third parties.
- To ensure the transparency in that process of examination and decision making, the government will publish an annual report on its overseas transfers, including the deliberation on how each decision was made.

10.5.2 The Mechanics and Decision-Making Process

One of the key features of the decision-making process regarding the transfers of defense equipment and technology is the due process and multilayered coordination on important cases. As seen in Fig. 10.1, the National Security Council (NSC), established in 2014, plays a key role in making decisions on important cases of defense equipment and technology transfer. The Ministry of Economy, Trade and Industry (METI) will conduct a first screening and make a *prima facie* decision. Any case that has precedence (i.e., the same or similar transfer of equipment and/or technology to the same destination was previously approved) will be decided as a routine case, but for a new case, the newly created Director-General (DG) level meeting will be convened to deliberate. Senior officials from the NSC, Defense, Foreign Affairs, and METI will take part in the process.

[29]The full text of the new Three Principles can be found at http://www.mofa.go.jp/files/000034953.pdf. The details and some cases of exemption, as well as prohibition, can be found at *Defense of Japan 2014* (also known as Defense White Paper) 329–331 (Japan Ministry of Defense 2014), available at http://www.mod.go.jp/e/publ/w_paper/pdf/2014/DOJ2014_4-1-3_web_1031.pdf.

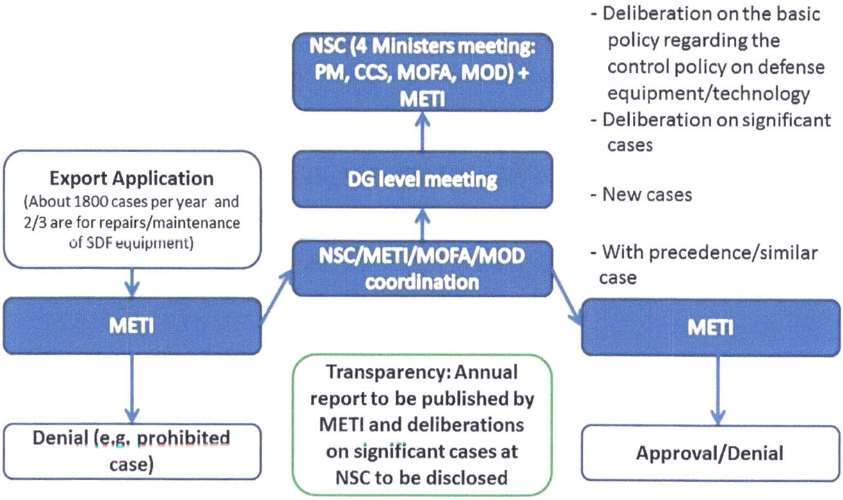

Fig. 10.1 Intra-governmental decision-making process regarding export licensing (Figure created by the author, based on the fact sheet of the Cabinet Secretariat, *supra* note 12, at 14.)

For a case of particular significance, the decision will be made at the NSC with the four key ministers and the METI minister in attendance. After the deliberation, the decision will be made public and the record kept. The first annual report of the transfers was issued on October 15, 2015.[30] In this report, it was explained that:

- Of 1841 cases of approval that was made,
- 1714 cases were regarding the repair and maintenance of SDF equipment, and
- 12 cases were regarding international joint development and production.

In addition, one case was approved by the NSC: that was the shipment of Patriot Missile PAC-2 seeker gyros to the United States.

10.5.3 Recent Developments

Since the change in the policy on defense equipment and technology transfer, a series of events have taken place reflecting the new policy. The following examples are some notable events:[31]

[30]The report is available (only in Japanese) at http://www.meti.go.jp/press/2015/10/20151015007/20151015007-3.pdf.

[31]For an overview of cooperation with the United Kingdom, France, Australia, and India, as well as capacity-building programs with Vietnam and other countries, see the briefing material prepared by the Ministry of Defense at http://www.mod.go.jp/j/approach/agenda/meeting/sobi-gijutsuiten/sonota/pdf/01/001.pdf (available only in Japanese).

- Japan has already signed bilateral agreements on transfer of defense equipment and technology with the United Kingdom, Australia, and France, and specific discussions on bilateral defense cooperation in the area of joint research and development are under way.[32] Japan also concluded similar agreements with India and the Philippines.[33]
- In addition to the leading case with Indonesia in 2006, Japan provided patrol boats to the Philippines[34] and Vietnam[35] to enhance their maritime capabilities.
- Further discussion on defense cooperation is under way with India.[36]
- The Japanese SDF have become more active since 2012 in extending capacity building programs to Asian countries like Vietnam, Mongolia, Cambodia, and others.[37]

10.6 Prospects and Challenges

Since the revision of Japan's policy is recent, it is premature to predict how this change would affect Japan's behavior in the relevant field of arms export and export control. Nevertheless, given its track record as well as constraints, some insights can be noted. First, it is highly unlikely that we will see any dramatic shift in Japan's participation in the global arms market, due to a generally cautious approach by both government and the private sector. This factor is multiplied by higher product cost and Japanese industry's lack of know-how and business models, compared with more competitive, already established arms manufacturers worldwide.[38] Joint research and development programs with US and European companies would be of much interest for the Japanese defense industry to pursue.

[32]See *Defense of Japan 2015* (Defense White Paper) 279–280, 288–289 (Japan Ministry of Defense 2015), available at http://www.mod.go.jp/e/publ/w_paper/pdf/2015/DOJ2015_3-3-1_web.pdf.

[33]The agreements were signed on December 12, 2015, and February 29, 2016, respectively.

[34]The bilateral exchange of notes was made on December 13, 2013, regarding the provision of the vessels, and the construction is currently under way. See http://www.mofa.go.jp/region/page22e_000048.html. It was reported that the first delivery would be made in 2016. See the article in *Nikkei Shimbun* (June 4, 2015) reporting on the winning of the bid by Japan Marine United (JMU) for building the vessels; the article is available (only in Japanese) at http://www.nikkei.com/article/DGXLASDE04H04_U5A600C1PP8000/.

[35]Japan decided to make necessary arrangements for providing newly built patrol boats to Vietnam. Since it will take some time to build and deliver the new vessels, Japan provided, as a temporary measure, used fisheries patrol boats, which arrived in Vietnam in February 2015. See http://www.mofa.go.jp/s_sa/sea1/vn/page4e_000195.html.

[36]*Defense of Japan 2015* (Defense White Paper), *supra* note 32, at 283.

[37]Id. at 276–277.

[38]Sato also points out the lack of experience of both Japanese business and government in arms exports. See Sato, *supra* note 2; and Research Group on Defense Production and Technology Platform, *supra* note 27, at 11.

Second, the government as well as the SDF will continue and expand bilateral collaboration in the security field, particularly with Asian countries on capacity building. This could include provision of training, joint exercises as well as transfer of limited equipment and technology. Besides enhancing the capacities of the other countries' armed forces, this cooperation will be an important step for confidence building and strengthening partnership in the region.

Regardless of the change in the policy, Japan will continue to adhere to the obligations of the ATT and other export control arrangements. The standards based on the new Three Principles for an application for an export license or technology transfer remain much stricter than the legal obligations stipulated in the ATT. What needs to be seen is how the Japanese government applies its treaty obligations. The position taken by many European Union (EU) members during the ATT negotiations could be a case in point. Many EU states that are major arms exporters advocated for the inclusion of strict standards for arms export in the ATT. This was not because they wanted to curb their own exports, but rather to differentiate their exports from those of states that may not consider human rights aspects in determining transfers of arms. While the number of arms transfers from Japan may not drastically increase in the near future in comparison to EU members, its decision-making process, rationale for the transfer and the standards to be applied deserve much attention.

10.7 Conclusion

Since the arms trade by itself is not inherently illegal, there is no reason to ban it totally. The current international trend is to set clear and shared standards on arms transfer, hold governments accountable for their transfers, and keep the transferred weapons under strict control and custody. In light of its new policy developments, Japan will also be required to set reliable standards to dispel any concerns about its transfers, especially through using the requirements set forth by the ATT. It is not yet certain if Japan's recent policy change is a mere reaction to the new regional and domestic environment, or a more fundamental shift in its strategic outlook and positioning on global security affairs. What is certain is that the change is based on the practical need to adapt the logistical foundation of the Japanese defense industry. The industrial necessity alone, however, could not prompt such a major departure from the previous policy. This change was made possible because of the increase in public support for Japan to engage in international activities in UN peacekeeping and other security-related programs, the expertise gained through such activities as well as the growing public awareness of the rapidly shifting security environment in the region. The subsequent decisions by Japan on specific transfers of defense equipment and their uses, especially the transfers to its neighbors, will determine how the public and the international community respond to this policy shift.

References

Ishigaki, Tomoaki. 2014. Defining the Future by Studying the Past: A Negotiator's Perspective on the Arms Trade Treaty. 57 *Japanese Yearbook Int'l L.* 371–414.

Wezeman, Pieter D., and Siemon T. Wezeman. 2014. *Trends in International Arms Transfers* (SIPRI Fact Sheet) 2015. Available at http://books.sipri.org/files/FS/SIPRIFS1503.pdf.

Wrubel, Wende A. 1989. Toshiba-Kongsberg Incident: Shortcomings of Cocom, and Recommendations for Increased Effectiveness of Export Controls to the East Bloc. *American University Journal of International Law & Policy* 4(1): 241–274 (winter).

Chapter 11
Export Control in the Arms Trade Treaty: Can It Have an Impact on the Prevention of Serious Violations of International Humanitarian Law?

Mika Hayashi

Abstract The export control scheme in the Arms Trade Treaty does not automatically help prevent serious violations of international humanitarian law. Its major challenge is the ambiguity of the terms used in the relevant provision, which allows for great latitude in interpretation by exporting states. Despite this challenge, compared to the extant frameworks, the Arms Trade Treaty is still the most focused export control for the purpose. In order to produce an impact on the serious violations of international humanitarian law, the States Parties to the Arms Trade Treaty should (1) foster transparency in their export control, and (2) adopt a very prudent approach when the importing states are countries of concern.

Keywords Serious violations of international humanitarian law (IHL) · Overriding risk · Transparency · Countries of concern

11.1 Introduction

The export control in the Arms Trade Treaty[1] provides an important means to help prevent serious violations of human rights law and international humanitarian law (IHL). It is certainly hoped that it makes a real impact on the prevention of such

[1]The Arms Trade Treaty entered into force on 24 December 2014. The UNTS number, normally used in a legal citation, is not yet available according to the UN treaty database (https://treaties.un.org/doc/Publication/UNTS/No%20Volume/52373/Part/I-52373-08000002803628c4.pdf, last accessed 6 January 2016).

M. Hayashi (✉)
Graduate School of International Cooperation Studies, Kobe University, Kobe, Japan
e-mail: nmika@kobe-u.ac.jp

D. Tamada and P. Achilleas (eds.), *Theory and Practice of Export Control*,
Kobe University Social Science Research Series,
DOI 10.1007/978-981-10-5960-5_11

violations. This note evaluates the export control of the Arms Trade Treaty from that perspective. Its main scope is evaluation of the impact of the treaty on serious violations of international humanitarian law.[2] This impact is necessarily limited given the ambiguities in the terms that constitute the provision on export control; they allow for a great latitude in interpretation by the exporting states. There is also an inherent problem of lapse of time in the export process. The note argues that, given these apparent challenges, the States Parties to the Arms Trade Treaty should (1) foster transparency in their export control, and (2) adopt a very prudent approach when the importing states are countries of concern. Since the purpose of this note is to evaluate the treaty's export control scheme, it does not discuss other challenges the treaty is confronted with, most notably its limited acceptance in terms of accession and ratification.[3]

11.2 Overview of the Arms Trade Treaty: Connection Between Arms Export Decisions and IHL

This section outlines the provisions of the Arms Trade Treaty and highlights the connection between the treaty and IHL. Detailed accounts of the treaty negotiations[4] and the treaty text[5] are available elsewhere.

The type of arms covered by the Arms Trade Treaty is conventional arms (Art. 2(1)). The UN Register of Conventional Arms is its predecessor, and the treaty adopted the seven categories set up by that register. A new category that was added is small arms and light weapons (Art. 2(1)(h)). Ammunition and parts are also covered by the treaty but are treated differently from the eight categories of arms provided in Article 2 (Arts. 3–4). The activities of the international trade that are covered are given the name *transfer*, which includes such activities as export, import, transit, trans-shipment, and brokering (Art. 2(2)).

The transfer of conventional arms is prohibited by the Arms Trade Treaty if the transfer results in violating the international obligations of the state that authorizes it (Art. 6). A transfer that contravenes an arms embargo imposed by the UN Security Council under Chapter VII of the UN Charter is a typical scenario under this article (Art. 6(1)). Any transfer that contravenes international obligations under any other international instrument is treated the same way (Art. 6(2)). In addition, a number of atrocities of unacceptable degree are listed as reasons for prohibiting a transfer: A state shall not authorize a transfer 'if it has knowledge at the time of authorization that the

---

[2]For a study that focuses on the prevention of serious violations of international human rights law, see Siatitsa (2015).

[3]As of March 2017, the number of States Parties to the Arms Trade Treaty is 92 according to the website of the Office of Legal Affairs of the United Nations (https://treaties.un.org/, last accessed 7 March 2017).

[4]See Holtom and Bromley (2013), Holtom (2014), Lustgarten (2015), Simonet (2015), Gro and Egeland (2015).

[5]da Silva and Wood (2015), Casey-Maslen et al. (2016).

arms … would be used in the commission of genocide, crimes against humanity, grave breaches of the Geneva Conventions of 1949, attacks directed against civilian objects or civilians protected as such, or other war crimes …' (Art. 6(3)).

Like Article 6, Article 7 also refers to several scenarios, and one of them is a serious violation of IHL (Art. 7(1)(b)(i)). The scenarios under this article are those that are not prohibited by Article 6. In these cases, Article 7 imposes an obligation of export control. First, it requires that if the export is not prohibited under Article 6, the exporting state is still under an obligation to 'assess the potential that the conventional arms … (b) could be used to (i) commit or facilitate a serious violation of international humanitarian law' (Art. 7(1)). Second, when there is such a potential, the exporting state can nevertheless consider the measures that can mitigate the risks that are identified (Art. 7(2)). Third, upon conducting the export assessment and considering the mitigating measures, if the exporting state still reaches the conclusion 'that there is an overriding risk of any of the negative consequences' just mentioned, the export shall not be authorized (Art. 7(3)).[6]

The treaty also has various provisions that could help ensure treaty compliance by States Parties: a recordkeeping obligation (Art. 12), a reporting obligation (Art. 13),[7] international cooperation (Art. 15), and international assistance (Art. 16). The treaty also makes or envisions a number of institutional arrangements, such as the Conference of States Parties (Art. 17) and the Secretariat (Art. 18).[8]

In sum, 'In requiring States to consider respect for IHL and human rights law in their arms transfer decisions, … the ATT aims to ensure that weapons do not end up in the hands of those who would use them to commit war crimes, serious violations of human rights and other serious crimes.'[9] The concrete expression in the Arms Trade Treaty is found in Article 6, prohibition of transfer in certain unacceptable cases, and in Article 7, the export control scheme, with the eventuality that the export is not authorized in certain cases. Both articles describe violations of IHL and international human rights law as reasons not to let the arms reach their intended destination.[10] Establishing this explicit connection between arms export decisions and IHL is a major achievement of the Arms Trade Treaty. As will be seen in Sect. 11.4, extant international frameworks are more general in their scope and nature; in those instruments, there is no explicit and concrete rule connecting arms trade decisions to violations of IHL.

---

[6]See Jørgensen 725–729 (2014) for more details regarding procedures under Articles 6 and 7.

[7]However, the First Conference of the States Parties in 2015 was unable to agree on the reporting template under this provision.

[8]A decision to set up the Secretariat in Geneva, Switzerland, was adopted in the First Conference of the States Parties in 2015. A detailed analysis of the institutional aspect of the Arms Trade Treaty is provided by Worster (2015).

[9]*Weapons: ICRC statement to the United Nations, 2015* (15 Oct. 2015), available at https://www.icrc.org/en/document/weapons-icrc-statement-united-nations-2015 (last accessed 26 November 2015).

[10]The Geneva Conventions, as well as protection from attacks against civilian objects and civilians in armed conflicts, referred to in Article 6, constitute an essential part of IHL.

11.3 Challenges for the Export Control Scheme in the Arms Trade Treaty

Can this export control scheme (Art. 7) in the Arms Trade Treaty make any impact on the prevention of serious violations of IHL? A quick answer is negative: the export control of the Arms Trade Treaty faces intractable challenges, and it does not easily or automatically prevent such violations.

(1) Ambiguous terms built into Article 7

The most obvious challenge in the export control scheme of this treaty is the ambiguity of certain terms used in Article 7. The scheme has to deal with 'the potential' that the arms in question could be used to commit or facilitate a serious violation of IHL and human rights law. How does one assess such 'potential'? Does the calculation change when one is dealing with a repressive and authoritarian regime? No guideline is provided in the provision. Then the scheme has to deal with measures that can 'mitigate risks' identified in this process. But how does one assess the mitigating effect of any measure, in particular, whether it is satisfactory or not in the context of the export control scheme? A program to monitor the stockpile that is jointly developed by the exporting state and the importing state is certainly good, but is it good enough? Again, there is no guideline to answer these and other questions. Then at the end of this assessment, if the exporting state determines that there is an 'overriding risk,' it is not allowed to authorize the export. An 'overriding risk' appears to be more than just an important risk or a significant risk.[11] That seems to be about the only criterion one can look to in determining what an 'overriding risk' is,[12] and it is frankly not much of a guideline.

On one hand, these ambiguous terms mean that there is a clear task ahead for each State Party, that is, 'translating the constructive ambiguity of the [Arms Trade Treaty] into law, policy and practice.'[13] However, one must also remember that Article 7 is worded and constructed in this way precisely because the exporting states wanted latitude in decisions regarding their arms export. The latitude allowed in each of the three steps of the export assessment described in Article 7 is a result of careful negotiation, and was agreed upon by the treaty negotiators. Rigorous, uniform, and objective application of this export control scheme is simply not expected.

Suppose there is a country called State A under an authoritarian regime, which has a record of violent internal repressions. The regime is believed to be stable, as such regimes tend to be. Under the Arms Trade Treaty, if State A wishes to purchase combat vehicles and assault rifles from manufacturers in a country called State B, the government of State B will carry out an export assessment in

---

[11]Lustgarten 596 (2015).

[12]See Gro and Egeland 219 (2015) and Casey-Maslen et al. 275–276 (2016) for different interpretations of 'overriding risk' by states that negotiated the ATT.

[13]Holtom 449 (2014).

accordance with Article 7. As a result of this assessment, State B may or may not conclude that there is a potential for committing or facilitating violations of IHL and international human rights law described in Article 7; the decision depends very much on what kind of information and factors are taken into account in the concrete assessment. If State B does not see the past pattern of repressions in State A as problematical, possibly as a sign that repressions may be repeated, the assessment will lead to a conclusion that the export can be authorized. If State B sees the stability of this authoritarian regime as a positive sign of a government that can handle the stockpile responsibly, this is also a factor in the assessment that facilitates the authorization of the export. Even when State B detects a potential for harm, if that harm is not considered an 'overriding' risk, State B will still authorize the export, again in accordance with Article 7. In sum, in this hypothetical situation, there is no guarantee that the export to State A will be denied under the export control scheme of the Arms Trade Treaty. More importantly, because of the ambiguous terms in Article 7, a decision to authorize the export in the case cannot be unequivocally characterized as unlawful.

(2) Challenge of lapse of time in the export process

Quite apart from the legal problem of ambiguous terms previously discussed, there is also a factual problem of lapse of time in the export process. Unlike the previous challenge discussed, this problem is not rooted in any treaty provision. It is rooted in a fact that a certain amount of time passes between the time of decision to authorize the export and the arrival of the exported items at the destination. Thus, a decision to authorize the export may be taken at a time when the importing state is largely peaceful and there appears to be no potential for IHL violations. It is possible, however, that the situation evolves very quickly after that decision and that, by the time the arms in question are in the hands of the importers, the importing state is, for example, in the middle of a civil war. The authorization of the export can of course be revoked at that point by the exporting state, but that is of little use regarding what may have already been shipped.

A recent case that illustrates this problem is the case of Libya from 2011 onward.[14] As the internal repression by the Qadhafi regime turned into a civil war, both the government forces and the rebels were accused of committing violations of IHL by a commission established by the Human Rights Council.[15] The United

[14]The civil war in Libya occurred prior to the entry into force of the Arms Trade Treaty, so the treaty itself is not applicable to the case. It is described here to illustrate the problem of lapse of time in the arms export process.

[15]See e.g. the evaluation of the International Commission of Inquiry on Libya, *Report of the International Commission of Inquiry on Libya*, A/HRC/19/68 (8 March 2012), paras. 119–120. Incidentally, the problem of lapse of time between a decision and an implementation is glimpsed in the work of this commission, too. Its original mandate, adopted before the start of the full-fledged civil war, did not include a reference to IHL. However, the commissioners felt such a need, and IHL was in fact used in the evaluation by the commission, Grace 41 (2015).

Kingdom revoked 72 licenses of arms export to Libya in the period 2011–2013.[16] Arguably an export decision made in good faith does not generate any responsibility for the exporting state (in the preceding example, the United Kingdom). The point this case illustrates is that the export control scheme of the Arms Trade Treaty may fail to achieve its objective even when it is carried out in conformity with the relevant provisions and in good faith.[17]

In sum, there are clear challenges. The export control scheme of the Arms Trade Treaty does not easily or automatically help prevent serious violations of IHL. In this regard, it is particularly important to remember that one of the major challenges in the export control scheme is the ambiguity of terms of the treaty itself, and that they are intentional; the states agreed to adopt these ambiguous terms in the description of the export control scheme. Therefore, the problem of the latitude given to the exporting states must be considered a given in looking for ways to make the export control scheme of this treaty as effective as possible.

11.4 Extant International Frameworks

There are a few previous international instruments that may also help prevent violations of IHL, or at least have been discussed as offering such a possibility by academic authors. Two branches of international law, namely, IHL and the law of state responsibility, will be examined in this section. The scope of each of these branches of international law reviewed in this section is not identical to the scope of the Arms Trade Treaty; nor is this section an exhaustive survey of relevant international instruments. Rather, this section serves to highlight a number of positive features of the Arms Trade Treaty by examining a few examples among extant international frameworks that cover similar goals.

(1) International humanitarian law

There is a duty to ensure respect for IHL. Under Article 1, common to the four Geneva Conventions,[18] states undertake not only to respect the Convention but to 'ensure respect for the present Convention in all circumstances'. According to the International Committee of the Red Cross (ICRC), this duty would mean, in the context of arms export, that 'All States have the responsibility to ensure respect for IHL not only in their development and use of new weapons, but also in their arms

---

[16]Committee on Arms Exports Control, *First Report: Scrutiny of Arms Exports and Arms Control* (2013), available at http://www.publications.parliament.uk/pa/cm201314/cmselect/cmquad/205/205ii01.htm (last accessed 7 January 2016).

[17]See also Article 7(4) of the ATT.

[18]Geneva Convention for the Amelioration of the Condition of the Wounded and Sick in Armed Forces in the Field, 75 UNTS 31 (Geneva Convention I) (Geneva Conventions II, III, and IV are omitted in this footnote).

transfer decisions.'[19] This is a position supported by a number of academic writers.[20] More generally, 'states, whether engaged in a conflict or not, must take all possible steps to ensure that the rules are respected by all, and in particular by parties to conflict'[21] under common Article 1. This is also an interpretation that was adopted by the International Court of Justice when it discussed common Article 1[22] in the context of the Fourth Geneva Convention.[23]

However, this duty to ensure respect for IHL is a very vaguely formulated duty.[24] It is difficult to determine a required or appropriate action under this obligation. In the context of the arms trade, the duty does not specify what should be done, or avoided, by exporting states when the destination of their export is engaged in armed conflict and violations of IHL are reported. A similar customary rule identified in a study under the auspices of the ICRC is also vague and therefore unhelpful, i.e. states 'must exert their influence, to the degree possible, to stop violations of international humanitarian law'.[25]

(2) Regime of state responsibility

In the regime of state responsibility, there is also a framework that could be used to make exporting states responsible for the consequences of their exports. This framework is often called 'shared responsibility' or 'complicity' and is found in Article 16 of the Articles on State Responsibility (ASR) by the International Law Commission.[26] In essence, this rule renders any state responsible that aids or assists another state in committing an unlawful act. In the context of arms transfer, an exporting state could be seen as an assisting, and therefore responsible, state if the exported arms are used by the importing state in the commission of an unlawful act, e.g. in the light of IHL.

However, according to the proponent of the ASR, the International Law Commission, the assistance to the unlawful act in this framework must be given *with a view to* facilitating the commission of the unlawful act,[27] and on top of that, it must actually do so.[28] This is a particularly high threshold from the perspective of holding any state responsible under this proposed rule.[29] Realistically, it is

---

[19]*Weapons: ICRC statement to the United Nations, 2015, supra* note 9.

[20]Brehm 368–375 (2007); Corten and Koutroulis 78–87 (2013).

[21]de Chazournes and Condorelli 67 (2000).

[22]Legal Consequences of the Construction of a Wall in the Occupied Palestinian Territory (Advisory Opinion) [2004] ICJ Report 136, 199–200, para. 158.

[23]Geneva Convention relative to the Protection of Civilian Persons in Time of War, 75 UNTS 287 (Geneva Convention IV).

[24]Focarelli (2010).

[25]Henckaerts and Doswald-Beck 509–513 (2005).

[26]Article 47 of the Articles on Responsibility of States for Internationally Wrongful Acts, reproduced in Crawford 272 (2002).

[27]Commentary to Article 16 (para. 5), reproduced in Crawford 149 (2002).

[28]*Ibid.*

[29]Aust 235 (2011).

extremely hard if not impossible to prove that the exporting state sold weapons to another state 'with a view to' facilitating the violation of IHL.[30] This requirement has to be modified if this framework of shared responsibility is to be of any help in prevention of violations of IHL. For example, a sufficient knowledge of violations that are committed by the use of exported arms, instead of the intention to help such violations, would be a more practical and helpful threshold.[31]

Another tricky aspect of the law of state responsibility is that it is a series of secondary rules that determine when a state is responsible for its unlawful act, and how the injured state can approach the responsible state. In other words, these rules are different from primary rules of conduct such as 'do not export' or 'do not authorize an export license'. According to the law of state responsibility, if the export decision is made unlawfully, the exporting state is responsible in the light of international law, and that is more or less the end of the story. In theory, an injured state is entitled to take a number of steps, including eventual countermeasures.[32] However, in a typical scenario where the export decision is linked to violations of IHL in the importing state, it is difficult to pinpoint the 'injured state' by this illegal decision.

In sum, a brief review of the two extant frameworks in this section indicates that these frameworks have only a very limited practical impact, if any, on arms export decisions and consequently on the prevention of violations of IHL. One also has to remember that these frameworks do not focus on the arms trade exclusively, but cover a much wider range of state conducts and situations. Against that background, the export control scheme of the Arms Trade Treaty is an instrument that specifically deals with arms export decisions and is explicitly set in the context of IHL, and that in itself is a great leap forward.[33]

11.5 Concluding Remarks

This note examined the export control scheme of the Arms Trade Treaty to determine whether it can have an impact on the prevention of serious violations of international humanitarian law. From this particular perspective, the Arms Trade

---

[30]Dominicé 286 (2010).

[31]Nolte and Aust 15 (2009).

[32]See Part III ('The Implementation of the International Responsibility of a State') of the ASR, reproduced in Crawford 254–305 (2002).

[33]Nevertheless the Arms Trade Treaty does not diminish the theoretical importance of the two frameworks reviewed in this section in the context of the arms trade. As noted in the UN treaty database, *supra* note 3, the number of States Parties to the Arms Trade Treaty is still limited. In contrast, the Geneva Conventions enjoy the adherence of 194 states, and Article 16 of the ASR has a definite potential to become a customary rule that binds all states. See Application of the Convention on the Prevention and Punishment of the Crime of Genocide [*Bosn. & Herz. v. Serb. & Montenegro*], [2007] ICJ Report 43, para. 420; Nolte and Aust 7–10 (2009).

Treaty is a move forward compared to extant international instruments, with its explicit connection between the arms export decisions and serious violations of IHL. At the same time, it is abundantly clear that the risk assessment of the export control scheme will not be carried out in a rigorous and uniform manner by all States Parties; the treaty itself is worded and constructed in such a way that a rigorous application is not possible, nor is it wanted by all those who negotiated the treaty text.[34] Against this backdrop, there are two recommendations that correspond to the two challenges identified in the present note.

(1) Transparency

Exporting states should make transparent what kinds of decisions are made according to what kinds of criteria when they carry out the assessment under Article 7. This transparency should allow the exporting states to try to copy the best practices observed. The transparency should also allow for constructive criticism of a decision that is too lax. The Arms Trade Treaty is equipped with a forum for reviewing its achievements, namely the Conference of States Parties. This institutional arrangement, together with the obligation of each State Party to render reports regularly, constitutes a good starting point to foster transparency.

However, these are not sufficient. The transparency needed in the export control scheme is of a kind that cannot easily be set up in formal reports or conferences. It is not merely the number of licenses given to exporters or revoked afterwards that has to be transparent. It is not merely the kinds of conventional arms and their destinations that have to be transparent. In the context of the export control scheme, what should be exchanged as information among exporting states is their concrete views of 'potential', 'mitigating measures', and 'overriding risk' in their specific export decisions.

In this regard, other regimes of arms control and disarmament have successfully exploited informal mechanisms to foster transparency, besides formal mechanisms such as the Conference of the States Parties.[35] Typically, the Conference of States Parties is a formal, annual meeting that is governed by the treaty provisions. However, as a mechanism to supervise the national implementation and to foster transparency of relevant decisions taken by each State Party, an annual conference that consists of a few days, with a long gap between one conference and another, is not the most effective forum. For that reason, other regimes of arms control and disarmament have come up with creative arrangements, such as intersessional meetings and networks that fill the gap between one Conference of States Parties and the next. These intersessional meetings are not governed by the treaty provisions, and that informality has proved to be of great benefit. Informality is flexibility. In terms of law, States Parties cannot be forced to attend such intersessional

---

[34]See also Lustgarten 594–595 (2015).

[35]This paragraph describes the summary of an argument regarding the Convention on Cluster Munitions and the 'Landmine Convention' by the present author, in Hayashi (2012, 2013), respectively.

meetings and are not obliged to disclose any details of their decisions in these meetings. In practice, however, these meetings form an essential part of the treaty regime and are taken seriously by those who participate in that regime, resulting in fostering transparency of the regime.

(2) A prudent approach for countries of concern

Exporting states should adopt a prudent approach in risk assessment when the export destination is a country of concern.[36] That is the only way to counter the factual problem of lapse of time. The situation of an importing state may evolve over time after a decision to authorize the export of arms is made; this is a natural event that cannot be avoided. That being the case, when an exporting state deals with a country that is of concern regarding its human rights record and possibly IHL record, the exporting state should take a prudent approach. The exporting state could, for example, look for extra mitigating measures and perhaps assurances from the importing state that it would not have sought had the importing state showed no signs for concern. The exporting state could, for example, informally obtain domestic and international experts' views on the country in question during the assessment. In sum, an exporting state could take a number of extra steps in its assessment in the case of export to a country of concern. There is no definition of a country of concern that is universally accepted; nevertheless, by looking at reports and views rendered and discussed by international bodies such as the UN Human Rights Council and various committees established under human rights treaties, it is possible to form an idea of countries of concern. Such a prudent approach is the only way to mitigate the problem of lapse of time. There is no leverage on arms that are already shipped and gone.

References

Aust, Helmut Philipp. 2011. *Complicity and the Law of State Responsibility*. Cambridge: Cambridge University Press.

de Chazournes, Laurence Boisson, and Luigi Condorelli. 2000. Common Article 1 of the Geneva Conventions revisited: Protecting collective interests. *International Review of the Red Cross* 837: 67.

Brehm, Maya. 2007. The arms trade and states' duty to ensure respect for humanitarian and human rights law. *Journal of Conflict and Security Law* 12 (3): 359–387.

Casey-Maslen, Stuart et al. 2016. *The Arms Trade Treaty*. Oxford: Oxford University Press.

Corten, Olivier, and Vaios Koutroulis. 2013. The illegality of military support to rebels in the Libyan War: Aspects of *jus contra bellum* and *jus in bello*. *Journal of Conflict and Security Law* 18 (1): 59–93.

Crawford, James. 2002. *The International Law Commission's Articles on State Responsibility: Introduction, Text and Commentaries*. Cambridge: Cambridge University Press.

da Silva, Clare and Brian Wood (eds.). 2015. *Weapons and International Law: The Arms Trade Treaty*. Brussels: Larcier.

[36]For this idea, see also Committee on Arms Exports Control, *First Report*, *supra* note 16.

Dominicé, Christian. 2010. Attribution of conduct to multiple states and the implication of a state in the act of another state. In *The Law of International Responsibility*, ed. J. Crawford, et al., 281–289. Oxford: Oxford University Press.

Focarelli, Carlo. 2010. Common Article 1 of the 1949 Geneva Conventions: A soap bubble? *European Journal of International Law* 21 (1): 125–171.

Grace, Rob. 2015. From design to implementation: The interpretation of fact-finding mandates. *Journal of Conflict and Security Law* 20 (1): 27–60.

Hayashi, Mika. 2012. The Convention on Cluster Munitions and the clearance of cluster munition remnants: Whose responsibility, and how to ensure effective implementation? *Journal of International Humanitarian Legal Studies* 3 (2): 322–343.

Hayashi, Mika. 2013. Clearance of remnants of war and its assistance as collective responsibility: The case of the Ottawa Convention (Mine Ban Convention). In *International Law in the New Age of Globalization*, ed. A. Byrnes, et al., 93–118. Leiden: Martinus Nijhoff.

Henckaerts, Jean-Marie and Louise Doswald-Beck. 2005. *Customary International Humanitarian Law*, Volume 1, *Rules*. Cambridge: Cambridge University Press.

Holtom, Paul. 2014. Arms Trade Treaty. In *SIPRI Yearbook 2014*, ed. Stockholm International Peace Research Institute, 445–450. Stockholm: Almqvist and Wiksell

Holtom, Paul and Mark Bromley. 2013. Arms Trade Treaty negotiations. In *SIPRI Yearbook 2013*, ed. Stockholm International Peace Research Institute, 423–431. Stockholm: Almqvist and Wiksell.

Jørgensen, N.H.B. 2014. State responsibility for aiding or assisting international crimes in the context of the Arms Trade Treaty. *American Journal of International Law* 108 (4): 722–749.

Lustgarten, Laurence. 2015. The Arms Trade Treaty: Achievements, failings, future. *International and Comparative Law Quarterly* 64 (3): 569–600.

Nolte, Georg and Helmut Philipp Aust. 2009. Equivocal helpers—Complicit states, mixed messages and international law. *International and Comparative Law Quarterly* 58 (1): 1–30.

Nystuen, Gro, and Kjølv Egeland. 2015. The potential of the Arms Trade Treaty to reduce violations of international humanitarian law and human rights law. In *Promoting Peace Through International Law*, ed. C.M. Bailliet, and K.M. Larsen, 209–226. Oxford: Oxford University Press.

Siatitsa, Ilia Maria. 2015. A serious violation of international human rights law: An attempt to clarify a crucial provision of the Arms Trade Treaty. *Journal européen des droits de l'homme* 5: 606–630.

Simonet, Loïc. 2015. *Le Traité sur le commerce des armes : Genèse, analyse, enjeux et perspectives du premier instrument juridique consacré à la réglementation des transferts internationaux d'armes conventionnelles*. Paris: Pedone.

Worster, William Thomas. 2015. The Arms Trade Treaty regime in international institutional law. *University of Pennsylvania Journal of International Law* 36 (4): 995–1076.

Chapter 12
Export Control in Space Activities

Setsuko Aoki

Abstract This article describes international frameworks as well as the EU and US laws and regulations on export control in space activities. First, the cross-border transfer of space-related goods and technologies is studied. Then, the question is answered if the space launch is regarded as export in the laws of the EU, US and Japan. Finally, reference to the on-orbit transfer of satellites is made from the export control point of view.

Keywords Wassenaar arrangement · ITAR · USML · CCL

12.1 Introduction

This chapter studies export control in space activities. In view of the present state of the exploration and use of outer space,[1] "space activities" are often defined as (i) the launch of space objects through outer space, (ii) the operation of space objects in outer space, and (iii) the reentry of space objects to Earth from outer space.[2] Prior to "space activities" in this sense, transnational transfer of goods (e.g., satellites) and technologies for space activities are carried out, for only a small number of countries have rockets (space launch vehicles) and launch sites for satellites as well as the capabilities to manufacture spacecraft.[3]

---

[1]"The exploration and use of outer space" is the term used in the United Nations (UN) treaties on outer space including the most important Treaty on Principles Governing the Activities of States in the Exploration and Use of Outer Space, including the Moon and Other Celestial Bodies (Outer Space Treaty), entry into force 10 October 1967, 610 UNTS 205.
[2]See, e.g., Setsuko Aoki, "2. Scope of Activity" (National Legislation Resolution of 2013), in Stephan Hobe, Bernhardt Schmidt-Tedd and Kai-Uwe Schrogl (eds.), *Cologne Commentary on Space Law*, Vol. III (Carl Heymanns Verlag, 2015), pp. 506–509.
[3]Only ten countries have autonomous launch capability as of January 2017.

S. Aoki (✉)
Keio University Law School, Tokyo, Japan
e-mail: saoki@ls.keio.ac.jp

D. Tamada and P. Achilleas (eds.), *Theory and Practice of Export Control*,
Kobe University Social Science Research Series,
DOI 10.1007/978-981-10-5960-5_12

Thus, international and national export control laws and regulations are studied according to the following order: (i) transnational transfer of space-related goods and technologies except that of rockets (on the earth), (ii) launch and reentry of space objects (between the earth and outer space), and (iii) on-orbit operations of space objects (in outer space). As Chap. 13 of this book deals with the export control regulations concerning missiles, which are almost identical to those relating to space launch vehicles, the concrete export control rules found in the MTCR will not be referred to in this chapter. Neither will be the transfer of the satellite-based data, as it is irrelevant from the export control point of view.

"Space object"[4] is the standard term used in the United Nations (UN) treaties on outer space, and means rockets, satellites and other probes as well as their parts and components. While this chapter uses "space object" as a general term, "spacecraft", "satellites", "payloads", etc. are also used as appropriate, for individual international frameworks and national laws use these terms.

12.2 International Frameworks for the Transfer of Space Objects

12.2.1 Export Control Systems of the Space Launch Vehicles and Related Items

12.2.1.1 Missile Technology Control Regime

There are no legally-binding instruments to regulate the transnational transfer of space launch vehicles (SLVs). Due to the technological similarity between SLVs and ballistic missiles, international transfer of the SLVs is subject to the legally non-binding export control framework of like-minded countries, or Missile Technology Control Regime (MTCR) established in 1987. Parts and component parts of SLVs as well as relevant technologies thereof which are outside the control by MTCR are regulated by the Wassenaar Arrangement. (The detailed exploration of the MTCR is found in Chap. 13 of this book.)

12.2.1.2 Wassenaar Arrangement

The Wassenaar Arrangement on Export Controls for Conventional Arms and Dual-Use Goods and Technologies (WA) was established in 1996 to prevent

---

[4]The definition of "space object" is found in the Convention on International Liability for Damage Caused by Space Objects (Art. I (d)) and the Convention on Registration of Objects Launched into Outer Space (Art. I (b)) as "[t]he term "space object" includes component parts of a space object as well as its launch vehicle and parts thereof".

destabilizing accumulations of conventional weapons through enhancing transparency and greater responsibility in transfers of conventional arms and dual-use goods and technologies.[5] Different from the MTCR, in case of the WA, it is the sole responsibility and national discretion of an each State to decide transfer or deny transfer of any listed items of the WA.[6] Such difference can be explained by the fact that the WA is not aiming at the non-proliferation of Weapons of Mass Destruction (WMD), and any State is entitled to obtain state-of-the-art dual-use items and arms to defend itself pursuant to Art. 51 of the UN Charter.[7]

Controlled goods, equipment, software and technologies in relation to space activities are specified in the List of Dual-Use Goods and Technologies comprising Category 1 to Category 9 items,[8] the Sensitive List and the Very Sensitive List, and also in the Munitions List.[9] Liquid, solid and hybrid rocket propulsion systems above a certain specifications specified especially in Category 9 (Aerospace and Propulsion),[10] in the Sensitive List[11] and the Very Sensitive List[12] as well as in the Munitions List[13] are subject to the export control through national laws.

12.2.2 Export Control Systems of the Satellites and Related Items: WA

There are no international rules and frameworks except the WA relating to space objects other than SLVs. International transfer of satellites, other space probes and relevant technologies thereof are regulated by the WA either as "spacecraft"[14] (Categories 7 and 9), "spacecraft bus"[15] (category 9), "spacecraft payload"[16]

---

[5]WA, Guidelines and Procedures, including the Initial Elements (12 July 1996 as amended) [hereinafter "Initial Elements"], I. Purposes.

[6]*Ibid.*, II. Scope, paras. 3–4 and 7.

[7]*Ibid.*, I. Purposes, para. 4.

[8]While this list is sometimes called "Basic List" to distinguish it from Sensitive List and Very Sensitive List, all of which are included in the same List of Dual-Use Goods and Technologies. See, *infra* note 9.

[9]List of Dual-Use Goods and Technologies and Munitions List, WA-LIST (15)1 Corr.1 (4 April 2016) [hereinafter "WA-LIST (15)1 Corr.1"].

[10]*Ibid.*, 9.A.5–9.A.10 (pp. 145–147).

[11]*Ibid.*, p. 163.

[12]*Ibid.*, p. 166.

[13]*Ibid.*, ML.20 b. (p. 197).

[14]This term is defined as "[a]ctive and passive satellites and space probes" in WA-List (15)-1 Corr.1, *supra* note 9, p. 219.

[15]This term is defined as "[e]quipment that provides the support infrastructure of the "spacecraft" and location for the "spacecraft payload"". *Ibid.*

[16]This term is defined as "[e]quipment, attached to the "spacecraft bus", designed to perform a mission in space (e.g., communications, observation, science)". *Ibid.*

(Category 9), or as items concerning "space-qualified"[17] found in Categories 3, 6, and 7 in the List of Dual-Use Goods and Technologies as well as in the Munitions List.

More concretely, specified in the List of the Dual-Use Goods and Technologies are space-qualified items such as solid-state detectors beyond a certain specifications,[18] space-qualified monospectral/multispectral imaging remote sensing sensors above a certain specifications[19] in Category 6 (Sensors and "Lasers"),[20] items on Global Navigation Satellite Systems (GNSS) in Category 7 (Navigation and Avionics),[21] and items specially designed to control actively the dynamic response or distortion of "spacecraft" structures, etc. in Category 9 (Aerospace and Propulsion).[22] In the Munitions List, the following items are examples under the regulation: spacecraft and its components specially designed for military use such as electronic countermeasure and electronic counter-countermeasure equipment,[23] electronic systems or equipment, designed either for surveillance and monitoring of the electro-magnetic spectrum for military intelligence or security purposes or for counteracting such surveillance and monitoring,[24] digital demodulators specially designed for signals intelligence,[25] GNSS jamming equipment and specially designed components therefor,[26] spacecraft and its components specially designed or modified for military use,[27] and Directed Energy Weapon (DEW) systems such as laser systems, particle beam systems and high power radio-frequency systems.[28]

The ninth Plenary meeting of the WA held in December 2003 approved that participating States would extend their national export control regulations to the non-listed dual-use items when the destination of such items are the State subject to a binding UN Security Council (UNSC) arms embargo, or any relevant regional arms embargo either legally binding on the exporting country concerned or in which it participates on a voluntary basis.[29] This is so-called "catch-all controls" implemented by other export control regimes including the MTCR. However, due to its intrinsic nature already mentioned, this has been applicable in much more

[17]This adjective is defined as "[d]esigned, manufactured, or qualified through successful testing, for operation at altitudes greater than 100 km above the surface of the Earth". *Ibid.*, p. 220.

[18]*Ibid.*, 6.A.2.a.1.a.–6.A.2.a.1.d. (pp. 97–98).

[19]*Ibid.*, 6.A.2.b. (pp. 101–102).

[20]*Ibid.*, 6.A.2.d., 6.A.4.c., 6.A.8.d., and 6.A.8.j. (pp. 102–122).

[21]*Ibid.*, 7.A.3. Technical Note a., 7.A.5. and 7.D. 5. (pp. 130–132 and 134).

[22]*Ibid.*, e.g., 9.A.10. c. (p. 147).

[23]*Ibid.*, ML 11.a. a. (p. 189).

[24]*Ibid.*, ML 11.a.c. (p. 189).

[25]*Ibid.*, ML 11.a.i. (p. 189).

[26]*Ibid.*, ML 11.b. (p. 189).

[27]*Ibid.*, ML 11.c. (p. 189).

[28]*Ibid.*, ML 19. (p. 196).

[29]Statement of Understanding on Control of Non-Listed Dual-Use Items, http://www.wassenaar.org/wp-content/uploads/2015/07/Non-listed_Dual_Use_Items.pdf (last accessed 4 February 2016).

relaxing manners than other export control regimes including in that each Participating State will determine at domestic level its own definition of the term "military end-use".[30]

12.3 Regional and National Frameworks for the Transfer of Space Objects

In this section, the EU and US export control frameworks concerning space-related items are depicted in some depth as laws and regulations of the EU and the US is the most relevant in considering space export control.

12.3.1 EU Frameworks

Council Regulation (EC) No. 428/2009 of 5 May 2009 setting up of a Community regime for the control of exports, transfer, brokering and transit of dual-use items (hereinafter "The EU Export Control Regulation")[31] is the foundation as the legally-binding export control regulations for EU countries.[32] As "export" is defined as the transfer of goods, software and technology from EU countries to "a destination outside the European Community",[33] it seems that launch of space objects is not included in export.

Authorization is required for the export of dual-use items listed in Annex I.[34] So is for a certain dual-use items not listed in Annex I;[35] this so-called catch-all controls is restricted in most cases against the risks contributing for disseminating WMDs and their delivery systems, but if the destination of the export is subject to arms embargo decided by the Council of the EU or the Organization for Security and Cooperation in Europe (OSCE) or imposed by a binding resolution by the UNSC, each State is required to carry out catch-all controls for military end-use.[36]

Space related items are enumerated in Category 3 (Electronics), Category 6 (Sensors and Lasers), Category 7 (Navigation and Avionics) and Category 9

---

[30]*Ibid.*

[31]http://eur-lex.europa.eu/LexUriServ/LexUriServ.do?uri=OJ:L:2009:134:0001:0269:en:PDF [hereinafter "The EU Export Control Regulation"] (last accessed 2 March 2016).

[32]This Regulation has been amended on several occasions including the amendment of the list of dual-use items (Annex I of the Regulation) in December 2011, May 2012, June 2014 and December in 2014.

[33]The EU Export Control Regulation *supra* note 31, Art. 2.2 (i)–(iii).

[34]*Ibid.*, Art. 3.1.

[35]*Ibid.*, Art. 3.2.

[36]*Ibid.*, Art. 4.1–4.5.

(Aerospace and Propulsion).[37] For instance, frequency synthesized signal generators with "space-qualified" atomic frequency standards (3A002),[38] "space-qualified"[39] solid-state optical detectors (6A002),[40] and receiving equipment for GNSS (7A105)[41] are among the controlled items used for SLVs and satellites. Examples of SLV-related items include SLVs (9A004), sounding rockets capable of a range of at least 300 km (9A104), liquid propellant rocket engines, systems or components thereof (9A105–9A106), solid propellant rocket engines (9A007, 9A107), production equipment for liquid and hybrid rocket propulsion systems and SLVs (9B115 and 9B116), and a certain technology for the use of SLVs (9E102).[42] The definition of "spacecraft" used in the EU Export Control Regulation is identical to that of the WA, which include a complete satellites (9A004), software specially designed or modified for the production of equipment for spacecraft (9D002).[43]

The EU Export Control Regulation does not have re-export control system different from that of the US.[44] Also different from the US system, the EU Regulation does not apply to the supply of services or the transmission of technology involving cross-border movement of persons.[45]

12.3.2 US Laws and Regulations

12.3.2.1 Two Lines of Export Control

Export of SLVs, satellites, parts and components thereof, as well as their technologies are subject to mainly two line of laws. One is the Arms Export Control Act (AECA)[46] and its regulations, or International Traffic in Arms Regulations (ITAR)[47] which contains the control list called the Munitions List (USML)[48] and

---

[37]The category number corresponds to that of WA.

[38]The EU Export Control Regulation, supra note 31, Annex I List, p.134.

[39]The definition of "space-qualified" is almost identical to that found in WA. *Ibid.*, p. 28.

[40]*Ibid.*, p. 180.

[41]*Ibid.*, p. 214.

[42]*Ibid.*, pp. 237–251.

[43]*Ibid.*, pp. 27, 237, 246.

[44]While the term "re-export" is used in the EU Export Control Regulation (Art. 2.2 (ii)), this means to export goods of non-EU countries to another non-EU countries before importing to EU countries. This is similar to reshipment or temporary landing in concept.

[45]The EU Export Control Regulation, *supra* note 31, Art. 7.

[46]22 USC Chapter 39, Public Law 94-329, Sec. 2751 *et seq.* (30 June 1976 as amended through Public Law 113-296 (19 December 2014).

[47]22 CFR Chapter I, Subchapter M (ITAR), Part. 120 *et seq.* (30 June 1976 as amended).

[48]*Ibid.*, Part. 121 [hereinafter "USML"].

the other is the Export Administration Act (EAA)[49] and its regulations Export Administration Regulations (EAR)[50] which contains the Commerce Control List (CCL).[51] The former governs the transfer of the defense articles and services and the latter, dual-use items which could be used for contributing to WMDs, their delivery systems as well as for military end-use.

Among the space-related items and technologies, transfer of SLV-related items has been inherently most strictly dealt with by the Directorate of Defense Trade Controls (DDTC) of the Department of State (DOS) pursuant to MTCR regulations, which is duly reflected in the AECA/ITAR,[52] and it has been next to impossible to export a complete SLV. In contrast, strictness of the transnational transfer of satellites, its parts, components and related technologies has been changed over the times under the US export control policy. This reflects most explicitly by the change of the licensing authority, which was sometimes administered by the Bureau of Industry and Security (BIS) [formerly Bureau of Export Administration (BXA)] of the Department of Commerce (DOC) which grants a license considering both US economic interests and other national interests,[53] and other times, by the DOS/DDTC which grants a license when the export in question does not compromise the US national security.[54] This section therefore describes the changes of the export control systems of satellites since the last decade of the 20th century to understand the characteristics of the US space export control systems.

12.3.2.2 Last Decade of the 20th Century: Changes of the Applicable Laws and Regulations from ITAR/USML to EAR/CCL and Again to ITAR/USML

Three Memorandum of Agreements between the US and China on commercial satellite launches from 1988–1989[55] enabled to launch US-made communications satellites from the Chinese territory.[56] Due to the gradual changes of the licensing

---

[49]50 USC Chapter 56, Public Law 96-72, Sec. 4601 *et seq.* (29 September 1979). EAA was lapsed on 20 August 2001 and the President, through Executive Order 13222 of August 17, 2001 has continued the EAR (see *infra* note 50) in effect under the International Emergency Economic Powers Act (IEEPA).

[50]15 CFR, Subtitle B, Chapter VII, Subchapter C, Part. 730 *et seq.*

[51]*Ibid.*, Part. 774 [hereinafter "CCL"].

[52]AECA, *supra* note 46, Sec. 2797 (d); ITAR, *supra* note 47, Part.121.1 (c); Category IV (Launch Vehicles, Guided Missiles, Ballistic Missiles, Rockets, Torpedoes, Bombs, and Mines); Part. 121.16.

[53]EAA, *supra* note 49, Sec. 3.

[54]AECA, *supra* note 46, Sec. 2751.

[55]China-US Agreements regarding Commercial Satellite Launches, done on 18 December 1988 and 26 January 1989. Entered into force 6 March 1989. *International Legal Materials*, Vol. 28 (1989) pp. 596–610.

[56]While US laws imposing sanctions against China were passed including the Foreign Relations Authorization Act for Fiscal Year 1990–1991 in response to Tiananmen, a series of presidential

jurisdiction for commercial satellites from the DOS to the DOC in the early 1990's to 1996, satellite export control to China was substantially liberalized.[57] Yet, the 1992 regulatory changes did not transfer all commercial communications satellites to the EAR/CCL, and satellites with (i) anti-jam capability, (ii) antennas with certain characteristics, (iii) intersatellite data relay links, (iv) space-borne baseband processing equipment, (v) cryptographic items controlled under the USML, (vi) radiation-hardened devices, (vii) certain on-orbit propulsion systems, (viii) certain attitude control and determination systems, and (ix) permanent orbit transfer engines (i.e. kick motors) remained under the ITAR/USML.[58] Such nine restrictions were formally removed and transferred to the licensing procedures pursuant to the EAR/CCL in October 1996.[59] At the same time, the licensing jurisdiction of technical assistance agreement (TAA) which enables to provide technical data on commercial communications satellites to foreign launch providers, was also transferred to the EAR/CCL.[60]

However, The US Congress found in 1999 that the illegally transmitted information to Chinese launch providers on the satellite-rocket interface data by the US satellite manufacturers through the launch accidents investigations[61] had improved Chinese missile capabilities. That Congress report resulted in a drastic change of the US export control policy. The licensing authority of all satellites was returned to the DOS/DDTC in March 1999,[62] and that situation lasted for the next 15 years.

12.3.2.3 US Export Control Reform: Back to the EAR/CCL

The latest export control reform started in August 2008, which delegated the Secretary of Defense and Secretary of State in October 2008 to carry out an assessment of the national security risks in case of the removal of the satellites,

(Footnote 56 continued)

waivers were granted under "national interest" determinations for export of US satellites for launch on Chinese SLVs. See, e.g., Select Committee, US House of Representative, *US National Security and Military/Commercial Concerns with the People's Republic of China* (declassified) (Report. 105–851) [hereinafter "Cox Report"] (March 1999), pp. 299–306.

[57]*Ibid.*, p. 301.

[58]Federal Register, Vol. 57, No. 206 (23 October 1992).

[59]Federal Register, Vol. 61, No. 215 (5 November 5 1996), pp. 56894–56896 (ITAR: hot-section technologies associated with commercial communications satellites, etc.; removal from USML for transfer to DOC/CCL).

[60]*Ibid.*, see, also, COX Report, *supra* note 56, p. 318.

[61]Satellites made by US Hughes Space and Communications and Space Systems/Loral experienced launch failures in 1992 and 1996 respectively in China. The necessary export control licenses such as TAA had not been obtained from the DOC/DDTC in the investigation process. See, e.g., Cox Report, *supra* note 56, pp. 224–296.

[62]National Defense Authorization Act for Fiscal Year 1999 [hereinafter "NDAA-99"], Public Law 105-261 (17 October 1998), Title XV, Sec. 1513 (a). It was effective on 15 March 1999 as specified in Sec. 1513 (c).

related components and technologies from the USML.[63] Based on its results and recommendations, the export control regulations provided for in the National Defense Authorization Act (NDAA) for Fiscal Year 1999[64] was repealed by the NDAA for Fiscal Year 2013.[65] It was decided that the licensing jurisdiction on commercial satellites would again be transferred to the DOC/BIS. The 2013 NDAA, however, specified that the prohibition of the export of satellites, etc. would be maintained to China, the DPRK, and any country that is a state sponsor of terrorism unless the President waives the prohibition on a case-by-case basis.[66]

On 24 May 2013, DOS/DDTC published a proposed amendment of the contents of the USML Category XV (Spacecraft Systems and Associated Equipment);[67] so did the DOC/BIS concerning the EAR/CCL on the same day.[68] Following the public comments and internal consultations, both the DOS/DDTC and the DOC/BIS published a respective interim final rule on 13 May 2014, the former as the revision of ITAR/USML Category XV,[69] and the latter as the revision to the EAR/CCL concerning spacecraft systems and related items.[70] Somewhat controversial and unsettled items such as certain remote sensing satellites and manned space sub-orbital vehicles were continuously discussed[71] until the final rules were published on 13 July 2015.[72] Interim final rules became effective as of 10 November 2014 for most of the proposed items, and "[C]larifications and Corrections" to the EAR (so-called "clean-up rules") was published in which clearer definitions and further explanations were given for certain rules which had previously been criticized as unclear.[73]

Items finally transferred to the EAR/CCL are specified below:

1. Communication satellites that do not contain classified components or capability;
2. Remote sensing satellites with performance parameters below certain threshold;

[63]National Defense Authorization Act for Fiscal Year 2010, Public Law, 111-84 (28 October 2009), Sec. 1248.

[64]NDAA-99, *supra* note 62, Sec. 1513.

[65]National Defense Authorization Act for Fiscal Year 2013, Public Law, 112-239, (2 January 2013), Title XII, Subtitle E, esp. Sec. 1261.

[66]*Ibid.*, Sec, 1261 (c).

[67]Federal Register, Vol.78, No. 101 (24 May 2013), p. 31444 *et seq.*

[68]*Ibid.*, p. 31431 *et seq.*

[69]Federal Register, Vol. 79, No. 92 (13 May 2014), pp. 27180–27189.

[70]*Ibid.*, pp. 27418–27443.

[71]*Ibid.*, pp. 27180–27189 and 27418–27443.

[72]Federal Register, Vol. 80, No. 133 (13 July 2015), pp. 39950–39957.

[73]Federal Register, Vol. 79, No. 218 (12 November 2014), pp. 67055–67059.

3. Systems, subsystems, parts and components associated with these satellites and with performance parameters below certain threshold of (1) and (2); and
4. radiation-hardened microelectronic microcircuits.[74]

The decision was made based not on the "article end-use", but on the "article capability" to protect critical technologies to the US national security.[75] Therefore, a satellite with the diameter of antenna greater than 25 m[76] or space-qualified optics with a largest lateral clear aperture dimension greater than 0.35 m remained on the USML even if those were for commercial use or used by a university satellite.[77] Likewise, while sub-orbital vehicles for space tourism are definitely for commercial use, its capability as a potential offensive weapon to attack the ground from space led to the conclusion that this could not be transferred to the DOC/BIS jurisdiction to the dissatisfaction of the space industry.[78]

Spacecraft systems including satellites that remain on the USML are equipped with better capabilities than a certain threshold regardless of their nature or purposes. A small number of the examples are: (i) spacecraft to automatically track space objects in real-time using imaging, infrared, radar, or laser systems; (ii) anti-satellite space vehicles; (iii) space-to-ground weapons system; (iv) attitude determination and control systems without using ground location points, better than or equal to five meters from low earth orbit (LEO); and (v) ground equipment for military spacecraft.[79]

As the 2013 NDAA specified, China remains included in Country Group D: 5. Countries in D: 5 Group are under the arms embargoes through the decision of the DOS, and even satellites under the DOC jurisdiction could not be exported to those countries unless the presidential waiver is granted. As of March 2017, 20 countries are in this category.[80]

Different from SLVs for which the internationally standardized export control measures exist, the change of the texts and operation of the US national laws concerning spacecraft directly affects the wide range of space activities as the US champions the all aspects of space activities.

---

[74]*Ibid.*, pp. 67058–67059; Federal Register, *supra* note 69, esp. pp. 27182–27189. Transfer to the EAR/CCL was effective as of 27 June only for the radiation-hardened microelectronic microcircuits, 45 days later of the announcement of the interim final rule. For the other items, it was 180 days later thereof.

[75]Federal Register, *supra* note 69, p. 27182.

[76]*Ibid.*, p. 27183.

[77]*Ibid.*, p. 27187.

[78]*Ibid.*, p. 27182.

[79]*Ibid.*, pp. 27186–17189, 27418–27443. See, also USML, *supra* note 48, Category XV (a) (1)-(21).

[80]EAR, *supra* note 50, Part 740, Supplement No. 1, pp. 7–8. Those countries include Afghanistan, DPRK, Iran, Iraq, Sudan, Syria and Zimbabwe.

12.4 Is the Launch of a Satellite Export?

No reference is made as to whether the launch is export and/or the reentry import in the international law instruments. That there is no rule on the definition and delimitation of outer space will not certainly help answering this question.[81]

US laws clearly answer this question, however. Prior to the 1984 Commercial Space Launch Act (CSLA),[82] the launch of SLVs and satellites was regarded as an export pursuant to the ITAR.[83] With the advice by the Senate Committee on Commerce, Science and Transportation, the CSLA provided that "[a] launch vehicle or payload shall not, by reason of the launching of such vehicle or payload, be considered an export for purposes of any law controlling exports."[84] Note that "payload" means in the US legislation that "an object that a person undertakes to place in outer space by means of a launch vehicle or reentry vehicle",[85] which is different from the definition of "spacecraft payload" in the WA.[86] Currently that reentry not considered an import is added in the US legislation.[87] Further as "launch" is defined to place or try to place a launch vehicle or reentry vehicle and any payload or human being from Earth to (i) in a suborbital trajectory, (ii) in Earth orbit in outer space, or (iii) otherwise in outer space,[88] the issue of the delimitation of outer space and air space for the purpose of export control is appropriately addressed.

As the Department of Transportation became responsible for the launch (and later also the reentry) for space objects, the ITAR has been amended since 1984 to provide that "[a] launch vehicle or payload shall not, by reason of the launching of such vehicle, be considered an export for purposes of this subchapter."[89]

Likewise, as already mentioned in 3.1 of this chapter, it seems that launch is not included in export by the EU Export Control Regulation, and perhaps, reentry would also be excluded from import.

As for Japan, as with the US and the EU countries, "export" does not seem to include the launch of space objects. "Export" is defined as transferring internal goods to any foreign States.[90] "Internal goods" means (i) goods (not foreign goods) situated in Japan and (ii) goods exploited on high seas by a ship of Japan's

---

[81]See, e.g., A/AC.105/1090 (30 April 2015) pp. 14–16.

[82]CSLA, Public Law 98-575 (30 October 1984). 49 USC. Sec. 2601 *et seq.*

[83]Valérie Kayser, Launching Space Objects: Issues of Liability and Future Prospects (Kluwer Academic Publishers, 2001), p. 113.

[84]CSLA, *supra* note 82, Sec. 2620 (b). Currently this provision is provided for in 51 USC, Sec. 50919 (f).

[85]51 USC, *supra* note 84, Sec. 50902 (13).

[86]See, *supra* note 16.

[87]51 USC *supra* note 84, Sec. 50919 (f).

[88]*Ibid.*, Sec. 50902 (7).

[89]ITAR, *supra* note 47, Sec. 120.17 (a)(6).

[90]Customs Act, Act No. 61, (2 April 1954 as amended), Art. 2 (2).

nationality.[91] As the area of "foreign States" is defined as "the area outside Japan",[92] at first glance, the launch of space objects could have been deemed as export. However, outer space is not included in the governmental notification of the places of destination for exports while the Antarctica and high seas are explicitly set forth,[93] it is now construed that the launch is not an export, and as corollary, the reentry would not probably be considered an import.[94]

12.5 Conclusion, or Remaining Issues: On-Orbit Transfer of Satellites

On-orbit transfer of ownership and operation of satellites has been an established phenomenon for almost two decades. This is deemed an export pursuant to the US ITAR as this provides that "[t]ransferring registration, control or ownership to a foreign person of any aircraft, vessel, or satellite covered by the US Munitions List, whether in the United States or abroad".[95] As for the US satellites transferred to the EAR/CCL, as "[a]ll US origin items wherever located"[96] are "subject to EAR",[97] as long as such items are to be transferred to a foreign national, it would be included in the export.[98] Therefore, all US satellites transferred to a foreign national shall be subject to US export control laws and regulations.

Finally, while it is not an export control regulation, mention should be made on the interesting example applied in the French Space Operations Act (FSOA). This Act provides that: (i) the transfer to a third party of the control of a space object (usually satellites) which has been authorized by the FSOA shall be subject to prior authorization; and (ii) any French operator intending to take the control of a space

[91] *Ibid.*, Art. 2 (4). "Japan" is defined as "Honshu, Hokkaido, Shikoku, Kyushu, and other dependent islands thereof specified by the Ordinance of the Ministry of Finance and the Ordinance of the Ministry of Economy, Trade and Industry" in Foreign Exchange and Foreign Trade Act (FEFTA), Act No. 228 (1 December 1949 as amended), Art. 6 (1)(i). Unofficial translation of the FEFTA is: http://www.japaneselawtranslation.go.jp/law/detail/?vm=04&re=01&id=21 (last accessed 3 February 2016).

[92] FEFTA, *supra* note 91, Art. 6 (1)(ii).

[93] Ministry of Economy, Trade and Industry (METI), Ministerial Notification Places of Destination Codes (10 August 2013), http://www.cistec.or.jp/service/cistec_teigen/meti_teigen2013/data/20131008-3.pdf (last accessed 3 March 2016).

[94] The Consumption tax relating to the launch of satellites from Japan has been exempted since April, 2006 based on the interpretation of the Consumption Tax Act that provides that transportation and communications of goods and tourists carried on between Japan and "outside Japan" shall not be subject to this Act. "Outside Japan" in this Act is not interpreted as the foreign States. See, Consumption Tax Act, Act No. 108 (30 December 1988 as amended), Art. 7(1)(iii).

[95] ITAR, *supra* note 47, Sec. 120.17 (a)(2).

[96] EAR, *supra* note 50, Sec. 734.3 (a)(2).

[97] *Ibid.*, Sec. 734.2 (a)(1).

[98] *Ibid.*, Sec. 734.2 (b)(1).

object whose launching or control has not been authorized under the FSOA shall obtain a prior authorization from the administrative authority.[99] The first case involves private transaction between French persons and from the French to a foreign national and the second case refers to get a control of satellite from foreign entity. This provision suggests the possibility of adequately supervising the on-orbit transaction of its nationals without directly using export control measures. As space exploration and use of outer space is unique in that States Parties to the Outer Space Treaty shall be directly responsible for its non-governmental entities,[100] authorization and supervision through national legislation is critical.

The least explored area of space export control is on-orbit transfer of ownership/control of space objects. Since increased transactions in this regard are found, the best way to address this should be studied both from the space law and export control law perspectives.

[99] Loi no. 2008-518 du 3 juin 2008 relative aux opérations spatiales (French Space Operations Act) (3 June 2008), Art. 3.

[100] Outer Space Treaty, *supra* note 1, Art. VI.

Chapter 13
Free Access to Outer Space Versus Export Control of Missiles

Yuri Takaya-Umehara

Abstract This article aims to explore the possibility of reinforcing the existing missile export control, the MTCR. Considering the growing number of states and non-state actors involved in launch activities, for both military and space missions, challenges to the MTCR have become diverse and more complicated to maintain its effectiveness. As SLV and ICBMs share the same technologies, Chap. 1 reviewed their legal basis for launch activities with an example of North Korea. Recognizing the dual-use nature of launchers, both SLV and ICBMs, Chap. 2 evaluated the achievements and highlighted shortcomings of the MTCR, and explored other possible elements that might serve to strengthen the regime.

Keywords ICBMs · Export control · MTCR · Space law · TCBMs

13.1 Introduction

With the increasing number of spacefaring states and private entities entering into the international market for launch services,[1] the proliferation of missile technologies has become a global concern more than ever. One of major reasons behind such a situation lies in the lack of multilateral legal instrument at the international level concerning the non-proliferation of the Inter-Continental Ballistic Missiles

---

[1]In 2015, launch service providers in 7 countries conducted 86 orbital launches, even not including launches for civil or military purposes. See, FAA, *Annual Compendium of Commercial Space Transportation*, Office of Commercial Space Transportation, 2016. Texts are available from: http://www.faa.gov/about/office_org/headquarters_offices/ast/media/2016_Compendium.pdf [Accessed: 22 February 2016].

Y. Takaya-Umehara (✉)
Kobe University, Kobe, Japan
e-mail: yuritakaya@hotmail.com

D. Tamada and P. Achilleas (eds.), *Theory and Practice of Export Control*,
Kobe University Social Science Research Series,
DOI 10.1007/978-981-10-5960-5_13

(ICBMs). In the 1960s, while the U.S. already recognized a potential threat that could be emerged by using the combination of Weapons of Mass Destruction (WMD) and ICBMs,[2] the former U.S.S.R. had kept providing military assistance including Scud-missile technologies to ambitious developing countries such as Afghanistan or Libya.[3] In the 1990s, their gap in understanding of the threat between superpowers resulted into a series of ICBM launching tests, carried out by those states suspected for the production of WMD.[4] Although such a situation was enough expected in 1991 when the former U.S.S.R. was dissolved with the spread of ICBMs to the third countries, the U.S. and other spacefaring states started the commercialization of outer space activities by encouraging private entities to get involved in launch services in order to reduce the launching cost. In the end, the existing regime, Missile Technology Transfer Regime (MTCR), has faced challenges to explore the possibility of preventing the proliferation of ICBM technologies, without impeding any national space activities. Considering that the MTCR is not a treaty, this article aims to evaluate the achievement of the MTCR and to identify its shortcomings. For this purposes, it consists of two chapters: the legal basis for launch activities [1]; and assessment of the MTCR [2].[5]

13.2 Legal Basis for Launch Activities

The legal basis for space launch activities is found in the Outer Space Treaty of 1967 (OST),[6] though, it defines neither outer space nor outer space activities, leaving a vagueness in the scope of its application. Among the five U.N. space treaties that provide the legal foundation regulating outer space activities,[7] only the

---

[2]Office of Technology Assessments, "*Technologies Underlying Weapons of Mass Destruction*," Federation of American Society, p. 217. Texts are available at: http://www.fas.org/spp/starwars/ota/934407.pdf [Accessed: 22 April 2016].

[3]Other states include Egypt, Iraq, North Korea, Syria, and Yemen. *See*, U.S. Congress, Office of Technology Assessment, *Technologies Underlying Weapons of Mass Destruction*, OTA-BP-ISC-115 (Washington, DC: U.S. Government Printing Office, December 1993), p. 217. Texts are available from: http://www.fas.org/spp/starwars/ota/934407.pdf [Accessed: 29 February 2016].

[4]A series of ICBM launching tests were conducted by Pakistan (April 1998), Iran (July 1998), India (April 1999), Pakistan (April 1999), and North Korea (1986, 1993, 1998, 2006, 2009, 2012, and 2016).

[5]The scope of this article focuses on missiles and rockets that are used for space launch activities as well as potentially capable to carry WMD, excluding smaller missiles not designed for those purposes.

[6]Treaty on Principles Governing the Activities of States in the Exploration and Use of Outer Space, including the Moon and other Celestial Bodies, 18 U.S.T 2410; TIAS 6347; 610 UNTS 205.

[7]Beside the Outer Space Treaty of 1967 and the Moon Agreement of 1979, the rests are followings: Agreement on the Rescue of Astronauts, the Return of Astronauts and the Return of

OST and the Moon Agreement of 1979 (MA)[8] contain specific provisions limiting military activities in outer space.[9] As the MA is not ratified by major spacefaring states, the OST falls in the scope of this chapter. According to Article IV, the deployment of Weapons of Mass Destruction (WMD) in Earth orbit and on celestial bodies, as well as their stationing in any outer space, are prohibited their stationing. In other words, Article IV allows the placement of conventional weapons in those areas and the use of Space/Satellite Launch Vehicle (SLV) for military mission. Contrary to the reaction of international community against the series of ICBM launch tests pursued by North Korea, the legal basis for the tests was claimed by the state that Article I of the OST provides freedom of outer space to all states.

Article I consists of three freedom: (a) freedom of exploration and use; (b) freedom of access; (c) freedom of scientific investigation of outer space[10] and space launch activities fall into the scope of those freedom. For example, Article I (1) stipulates that "[T]he exploration and use of outer space, including the Moon and other celestial bodies, shall be carried out for the benefit and in the interests of all countries, irrespective of their degree of economic or scientific development, and shall be the province of all mankind." Thus, the provision explicitly allow all states, including non-state party, to enjoy the space launch activities and already becomes customary international law.[11] It is designed to have a lead function in the rest of OST provisions by bringing the notion of the "province of all mankind," while it also serves to regulate outer space activities by specified limitations.[12]

Using this legal basis, North Korea has continued its ICBM launching tests. In 1998, it carried out the test towards Japan with an explanation that it was rocket launch test under the freedom of outer space stipulated in Article I of OST. However, in response to its repeated tests in 2006, criticisms from the international community led to the endorsement of the UN Security Council resolution 1695[13] requiring North Korea to stop ICBM tests as well as called for all states to stop missile-related export and import. The resolution of 1695 reinforced the previous one, UN Security Council resolution 1540 of 2004[14] which firstly affirmed ICBMs

(Footnote 7 continued)

Objects Launched into Outer Space, 19 U.S.T 7570; TIAS 6599; 672 UNTS 119; Convention on International Liability for Damage Caused by Space Objects, 24 U.S.T 2389; TIAS 7762; 961 UNTS 187; Convention on Registration of Objects Launched into Outer Space, 28 U.S.T 695; TIAS 8480; 1023 UNTS 15.

[8]Agreement Governing the Activities of States on the Moon and Other Celestial Bodies, 18 ILM 1434; 1363 UNTS 3.

[9]Tronchetti (2015).

[10]*Ibid.*, pp. 34–37.

[11]Sugihara (2008).

[12]Hobe et al. (2009).

[13]UNSC S/RES/1695(2006), 15 July 2006.

[14]UNSC Res. S/RES/1540 (2004), 28 April 2004. It aims at non-state actors that attempt to develop, acquire, manufacture, possess, transport, transfer or use WMD and their means of delivery.

as "WMD's delivery means" putting ICBMs into the framework for the non-proliferation of WMD, with extending the scope from states to non-state actors that attempt to develop, acquire, manufacture, possess, transport, transfer or use WMD and "their means of delivery". Thus, those resolutions prevented North Korea from maintaining its position that a series of launch tests fall into the scope of its freedom in outer space under the Article I of OST. Then, how should be the freedom interpreted in terms of ICBM tests?

The term "freedom" in Article I means that any entity who benefits from the freedom does not need to ask for permission from other governments over its exploration and use of outer space.[15] The provision neither clarifies what kind activities fits in the scope of freedom nor explicitly prohibits the use of ICBMs for the deployment of space objects in orbit around the Earth. In sum, North Korea does not need any permission from any other governments for "rocket" launch tests, which are part of national space activities. However, in fact, North Korea enhanced its capabilities of ICBMs after a series of launch tests; therefore, such ICBM launch tests need to be examined under the UN Charter, in accordance with Article I (2) and Article III of OST.

Article I (2) stipulates that outer space are free for exploration and use by all states in accordance with international law, and Article III follows it by adding the terms "including the Charter of the United Nations." In the drafting process of UN General Assembly resolution of 13 December 1963, the U.S. expressed its position that military activity is permissible provided that it is in accordance with the UN Charter and that military preparations are permitted by the right of self-defense under Article 51 of the UN Charter.[16] In this respect, non-UN organization, the Conference on Disarmament considered the right of self-defense in outer space in the Committee for the Prevention of an Arms Race in Outer Space (PAROS Committee). On the contrary to the U.S. position, it concluded that the right of self-defense cannot be exercised in outer space as that UN General Assembly resolution 39/59 of 12 December 1984, which first referred to the use of force in outer space, "[*R*]*ecalls* the obligation of all States to refrain from the threat or use of force in their space activities".[17] Thus, the legal basis for rocket launch activities and ICBM launch tests differs presenting challenges to the exiting regime over missile export control.

In sum, the legal basis for SLV launch activities is in the freedom of outer space activities stipulated in Article I of OST, which does not provide such a basis for ICBM launch tests to North Korea. Taking it into consideration, the following chapter examines the existing regime, the MTCR.

[15]S. Hobe, B. Schmidt-Tedd, K.-U. Schrogl and G. r. M. Goh, *supra* note 12, p. 34.

[16]I. Brownlie (1966).

[17]UNGA Res. A/RES/39/59, "Prevention of an arms race in outer space," 12 December 1984.

13.3 Assessment of the MTCR

It is technologically difficult to draw a line between SLV and ICBMs, which accelerates the proliferation of ICBM technologies. For example, the number of spacefaring states capable of launching satellites in orbit is 9; while that of states possessing ICBM capabilities is 34 as of April 2016.[18] Considering such a complexity in missile export control, the present chapter first outlines the overview of the MTCR [2.1] and evaluate its effectiveness by tracing current development [2.2] in order to highlight its shortcomings [2.3] and concludes with other elements that serve to strengthen the MTCR [2.4].

13.3.1 Overview

In 1987, the exiting regime for missile export control, the MTCR,[19] was established by the U.S. and other agreed G-7 countries.[20] It aims to limit the risks of WMD proliferation by controlling transfers that could make a contribution to delivery systems for such weapons.[21] As of 2017, 35 member states[22] agreed to work for the goal through their coordination of national export controls under the MTCR Guidelines,[23] and to strengthen another regime under the Nuclear Non-Proliferation Treaty of 1968.[24] Longer range ballistic and cruise missiles with ranges over 300 km and payloads over 500 kg[25] are strictly prohibited to be transfer to non-member states; while the Guidelines are not designed to impede national space

[18]MTCR, "MTCR Partners." Texts are available from: http://www.mtcr.info/english/partners.html/ [Accessed: 20 February 2016].

[19]Agreement on Guidelines for the Transfer of Equipment and Technology Related to Missiles (hereinafter MTCR Agreement), 16 April 1987; 26 ILM 599 (1987).

[20]U.S. Congress, Office of Technology Assessment, *supra* note 3, p. 1199. Original member states are: Canada, France, Germany, Italy, Japan, the United Kingdom and the United States.

[21]MTCR, "Introduction: The Missile Technology Transfer Regime (MTCR) - MTCR Annex Handbook," p. vi. Texts are available at: http://www.mtcr.info/english/MTCR_Annex_Handbook_ENG.pdf. [Accessed: 29 April 2016].

[22]35 member states are: Argentina, Australia, Austria, Belgium, Bulgaria, Brazil, Canada, Czech Republic, Denmark, Finland, France, Germany, Greece, Hungary, Iceland, India, Ireland, Italy, Japan, Luxembourg, Netherlands, New Zealand, Norway, Poland, Portugal, Republic of Korea, Russian Federation, South Africa, Spain, Sweden, Switzerland, Turkey, Ukraine, United Kingdom and United States. India is the latest member state that joined in 2016.

[23]MTCR, "Guidelines for Sensitive Missile-Relevant Transfer." Texts are available from: http://www.mtcr.info/english/guidetext.html [Accessed: 28 February 2016].

[24]Treaty on the Non-Proliferation of Nuclear Weapons (Non-Proliferation Treaty), London/Moscow/Washington, 1 July 1968; 729 UNTS 161; TIAS 6839; 21 U.S.T 483; UKTS 1970 No. 88; Cmnd. 3683; ATS 1973 No. 3; 7 ILM 809 (1968).

[25]The scope does not cover manned aircraft.

programs or international cooperation in such programs as long as they could not contribute to WMD's delivery systems.

Like other export control regimes for the WMD non-proliferation,[26] the MTCR is not a treaty but a set of voluntary arrangements among agreed states.[27] In order to maintain its effectiveness by covering SLV, the MTCR places the export of space launch vehicles, components and the production technologies used in civil space programs under strict controls.[28] The whole goods to control are listed in the MTCR Equipment, Software and Technology Annex[29] that divide all missile-related technologies into Category I and II.

Category I items include "complete rocket and unmanned aerial vehicle systems (including ballistic missiles, space launch vehicles, sounding rockets, cruise missiles, target drones, and reconnaissance drones), capable of delivering a payload of at least 500 kg to a range of at least 300 km, their major complete subsystems (such as rocket stages, engines, guidance sets, and re-entry vehicles) and related software and technology, as well as specially designed production facilities for these items." The items in Category I are prohibited to transfer regardless of the purpose of the export and rarely licensed for export.[30] Furthermore, the specifically designed production facilities for those systems are also prohibited without exception.[31]

As to SLV, there are 20 states[32] recognized under the MTCR as producing complete rocket systems and self-contained flight vehicles that, as well as sounding rockets, are used to place satellites in Earth orbit to gather satellite-based data. Then, the difference between those systems and offensive ballistic missiles is in their payload and intended use[33] and the addition of a weapons payload and different guidance algorithms enable SLV and sounding rockets to be used as ballistic missiles.[34] Thus, technological difference is neither clarified in the MTCR nor defined in any other documents for export control.

---

[26]The other regimes are: the Nuclear Suppliers Group (NSG); the Australia Group (AG); and the Wassenaar Arrangement (WA).

[27]Inter-sessional consultations take place monthly through Point of Contact (POC) meetings in Paris, while Technical Experts Meetings, Information Exchanges, and Licensing and Enforcement Experts Meetings are held annually. As the MTCR has no secretariat; distribution of the Regime's working papers is carried out through the POC in support of the Ministry of Foreign Affairs of France. See, MTCR, *supra* note 21.

[28]F. Tronchetti, *supra* note 9, p. 361.

[29]MTCR Equipment, Software and Technology Annex (hereinafter MTCR Annex), 23 October 2012. Texts are available at: http://www.mtcr.info/english/annex.html [Accessed: 21 April 2016].

[30]P.V. Fenema (2015).

[31]See, "Introduction, Definition, Terminology," Sec. 2, Definitions, MTCR Annex, *supra* note 29.

[32]Those states are: Brazil, Canada, China, Egypt, France, Germany, India, Iran, Israel, Italy, Japan, North Korea, Pakistan, Russian Federation, South Korea, Spain, Syria, Ukraine, United Kingdom, United States.

[33]MTCR, *supra* note 21.

[34]MTCR, *supra* note 21.

13.3.2 Current Developments

The scope of the MTCR has been extended with the increase of member states. When the MTCR was established in 1987, its focus was on the non-proliferation of nuclear weapons. In 1992 the Gulf War urged the MTCR to add biological and chemical weapons into the scope. Facing a need to control smaller rockets and missiles, in 2002, substantial improvement was made to Category II by including "Item 19. Other Complete Delivery Systems" to cover: (1) complete rocket systems with the range less than 300 km; (2) complete unmanned aerial vehicle systems (including cruise missile systems, target drones and reconnaissance drones); (3) complete unmanned aerial vehicle systems with: (a-1) an autonomous flight control and navigation capability; or (a-2) capability of controlled flight out of the direct vision range involving a human operation; and (b-1) incorporating an aerosol dispensing system/mechanisms with a capacity greater than 20 L; or (b-2) designed or modified to incorporate an aerosol dispensing system/mechanisms with a capability of greater than 20 L; and (4) the "intention" as an element for the evaluation to transfer. Furthermore, in 2003, lessons from the Australia Group led to the introduction of "catch-all-control" to check the end-user of the export.

Not only extending the scope of items to control, the MTSR membership was also reviewed and achieved the following outcomes: (1) Argentina, Egypt, and Iraq abandoned their joint Condor II ballistic missile program; (2) Brazil, South Africa, South Korea, and Taiwan also shelved or eliminated missile or space launch vehicle programs; (3) some Eastern European countries, such as Poland and the Czech Republic, destroyed their ballistic missiles, in part, to better their chances of joining MTCR; and (4) Missile efforts have been discouraged in Libya and Syria.[35] However, in contrast to those accomplishment, the following facts still remain unsolved: (1) Iran, India, North Korea, and Pakistan continue to advance their missile programs; (2) India is testing missiles in the intercontinental range; (3) North Korea and Iran would become sellers rather than simply buyers on the global arms market.[36] Considering that India joined the MTCR in 2016, achievements need to be evaluated by individual state.

13.3.3 Shortcomings

There are several shortcomings in the MTCR mechanisms as follows: (1) non-binding nature; (2) the principle of consensus in decision-making; (3) continuous breaches by non-member state who made a commitment to comply with the MTCR; and (4) its loophole revealed by emerging new styles of launch activities such as air-launch.

---

[35]K. Davenport (2015).

[36]K. Davenport, *ibid*.

As to (1), as mentioned above, the MTCR is not a treaty that results into the lack of verification mechanisms to ensure its compliance. As to (2), the principle of consensus in decision-making reduces the flexibility in enlarging or strengthening the regime, though it should maintain its effectiveness by excluding undesirable states. For example, in 2015, India applied for the membership but a consensus was blocked by Italy during the October 2015 Plenary though was welcomed to the regime in 2016. In this respect, it should be noted that the principle of consensus does not influence on any bilateral decision such as the U.S.-South Korea Agreement of 2012 that the U.S. allowed South Korea to extend the range of a ballistic missiles from 500 to 800 km in 2017.[37] As to (3), the effectiveness of the regime has been reduced by the continuous breaches of non-member states that declared their compliance with the regime. China, Israel, Romania, and the Slovak Republic have agreed to observe MTCR Guidelines as "unilateral adherents."[38] Israel, who declared its compliance with the Guidelines, completed a memorandum of understanding with the U.S.[39] Considering that, within a decade after creation of the MTCR, 9 states who were recognized as potential threats already acceded to the MTCR Guidelines to become member states. In this respect, the effectiveness of the MTCR should be highly evaluated,[40] while there are still some non-member states that attract attention in the international community by revealing a weakness of the MTCR, for example, China.

Although China first promised tentatively to abide by the MTCR in 1991 and 1992 and later reaffirmed its commitment in the joint statement of 1994 with the U.S.,[41] it continuously breaches the MTCR Guidelines by assisting Iran and North Korea that has been reported publicly since 1998.[42] In 2004, China applied for the MTCR membership; however, due to its continuous transfer of the listed items to Pakistan, Iran, and North Korea without informing the MTCR member states,[43] its application was rejected.[44] Due to the vagueness in its compliance, China officially committed again to the MTCR goals by adopting its own internal legislations and organizational structures in 2008.[45] However, in 2012, it was revealed that China exported bauxite (aluminum ore), a material that could be used to manufacture missiles, to a weapons plant in North Korea.[46] With its violations of UN Security Council resolutions, China's performance raised a great concern and highlighted the need for a treaty in the non-proliferation of WMD's delivery means.

---

[37]K. Davenport (2012).

[38]Nikitin et al. (2012).

[39]M.B. Nikitin, P.K. Kerr and S,A. Hildreth, *ibid.*

[40]Joyner (2009).

[41]Kan (2015).

[42]S.A. Kan, *ibid.*, pp. 18–19.

[43]Grimmett (2010).

[44]See, S.A. Kan, supra note 41.

[45]M.B. Nikitin, P.K. Kerr and S.A. Hildreth, supra note 38.

[46]S.A. Kan, *supra* note 41, p. 19.

Last, as to (4), the loophole of the MTCR is highlighted by the emerging new model of launch activities such as air-launch. Air-launch uses the combination of a carrier aircraft and a small rocket to deliver small satellite in low earth orbit (LEO). The carrier aircraft is designed as normal manned aircraft and departs from airport/spaceport, equipped with a small rocket for the second launch at an altitude of 8–10 km. There are already several space-faring states starting air-launch programs[47] for commercial purposes. However, the introduction of air-launch to international market reveals two shortcomings of the MTCR. First the small rocket used for air-launch falls into Category II, not Category I, that are examined case by case, even though the carrier aircraft with a smaller rocket is capable of delivering a payload to a range of 300 km, which falls into Category I. Second, the carrier aircraft uses a pilot. As both Category I and II only target Unmanned Aerial Vehicles (UAVs), the carrier aircraft does not fall in the scope of the MTCR. Furthermore, although those air-launch activities are mainly for civil or commercial purposes, it is hard to deny any possibility for cooperation over missile R&D or commercial Expendable Launch Vehicles (ELVs) which could contribute to WMD delivery systems.[48]

In sum, shortcomings in the MTCR need to be reviewed to maintain its effectiveness following new style of space launch activities. To explore any possibility to reinforce the existing MTCR, other possible elements are introduced in the following section.

13.3.4 Other Elements to Reinforce the MTCR

There are other elements that serve to strengthen the MTCR as follows: (1) Hague Code of Conduct against Ballistic Missile Proliferation of 2002 (HCoC)[49]; (2) a series of UN Security Council resolutions against North Korea's launch tests; and (3) Transparency and Confidence-Building Measures (TCBMs) in outer space activities.

First, the HCoC was launched in 2002 after the MTCR Plenaries in Helsinki and Ottawa held respectively in 2000 and 2001. In order to prevent and curb the proliferation of ballistic missiles systems capable of delivering WMD, complementarily the creation of HCoC was initiated by the MTCR member states. The HCoC members commit themselves to notify others on launches and test flights of

[47]DARPA-Airborne Launch Assist Space Access program by U.S.; STARLAB program by U.S.; Polyot program by Russia, Germany, Ukraine and Indonesia; NLR Air-Launch by The Netherlands; Yuzhnoye UAV program by Ukraine; and three U.S. companies started feasibility studies: Virgin Galactic, Stratolaunch System Inc., Boeing.

[48]P.V. Fenema, *supra* note 30, p. 419.

[49]To learn further developments and achievements about HCoC, see the following website *Nuclear Threat Initiative*. Texts are available at: http://www.nti.org/learn/treaties-and-regimes/hague-code-conduct-against-ballistic-missile-proliferation-hcoc/ [Accessed: 19 March 2017].

ballistic missile and space launch vehicles, as well as to submit an annual declaration of their national policies on ballistic missiles and space launch vehicles.[50]

Beside the HCoC, a series of UN Security Council resolutions against the proliferation of WMD and its delivery systems reinforce the MTCR. Through UN Security Council resolution 1718 of 2006,[51] resolution 1874 of 2009,[52] resolution 2087 of 2013,[53] resolution 2094 of 2013,[54] and resolution 2270 of 2016,[55] international community strongly condemn North Korea's launch tests. Different from the MTCR, those resolutions focus on a specific state with sanctions under national export control of UN member states.

Last, the application of TCBMs in outer space activities[56] to missiles export control is worth exploring the possibility of strengthening the MTCR effectiveness. As the original concept and function of TCBMs are traceable to Confidence-Building Measures (CBMs)[57] in the law of disarmament and arms control that aim to strengthen the compliance mechanisms, the application of TCBMs to the MTCR provides another option to enhance transparency in launch activities for the same purpose.[58]

---

[50]See the statement by the MTCR Chair, Ambassador Piet de Klerk, "The Missile Technology Control Regime: Successful international co-operation, with limits," The 23rd Asian Export Control Seminar, Tokyo, 23–25 February 2016. Texts are available at: http://www.mtcr.info/english/160228%20Presentation%20MTCR%20for%20AECS2016.pdf [Accessed: 20 April 2016].

[51]UNSC, S/RES/1718 (2006), 14 October 2006.

[52]UNSC, S/RES/1874 (2009), 12 June 2009.

[53]UNSC, S/RES/2087 (2013), 22 January 2013.

[54]UNSC, S/RES/2094 (2013), 7 March 2013.

[55]UNSC, S/RES/2270 (2016), 2 March 2016.

[56]The concept of transparency in outer space activities was firstly introduced in the 1990 s when the application of Confidence-Building Measures (CBMs) to outer space was considered in the context of the prevention of an arms race in outer space (PAROS). Although intensive work of the Group of Governmental Experts (GGE) was not resulted into any international instrument, the same concept was again brought up in the UN by Russia in 2005. While U.S. prioritized national security in outer space activities after *September 11* in 2001, pursuing Missile Defense, Russia started claiming the need for transparency in outer space by submitting to the General Assembly. After the endorsement of a series of UN resolutions "Transparency and Confidence-Building Measures in Outer Space Activities," Russia has initiated a treaty-making process in cooperation with China. On the other hand, the Council of Europe launched the international code of conduct on outer space activities in 2008, though U.S. denies any possibility of the code creating any treaty nor customary international law.

[57]UNGA Res. A/RES/43/78 H, "Guidelines for Confidence-Building Measures," 7 December 1988.

[58]See, Y. Takaya-Umehara (2010).

13.4 Conclusion

With the growing number of states and non-state actors involved in launch activities, for both military and space missions, challenges to the MTCR have become diverse and more complicated to maintain its effectiveness. As SLV and ICBMs share the same technologies, Chap. 1 reviewed their legal basis for launch activities with an example of North Korea. Recognizing that all states are entitled to pursue SLV launch activities under Article I of the OST, Chap. 2 evaluated the achievements and highlighted shortcomings of the MTCR, and explored other possible elements that might serve to strengthen the regime. In the last section of Chap. 2, the application of TCBMs to the MTCR was addressed to make a balance between legal SLV launch activities and non-binding missile export control. In conclusion, due to the lack of binding force of the MTCR, it needs to work with other instruments such as HCoC or TCBMs which are related to launch activities of both SLV and ICBMs.

References

Brownlie, I. 1966. *Principles of Public International Law*, 236. Oxford University Press.

Davenport, K. 2012. "South Korea Extends Missile Range". *Arms Control Association*. Texts are available at: https://www.armscontrol.org/act/2012_11/South-Korea-Extends-Missile-Range [Assessed: 13 April 2016].

Davenport, K. 2015. "The missile technology control regime at a glance". *Arms Control Association*. Texts are available at: http://www.armscontrol.org/print/2596. Assessed: 18 Apr 2016.

Fenema, P.V. 2015. "Legal aspects of launch services and space transportation". In *Handbook on Space Law*, ed. Frans von der Dunk and Fabio Troncetti, 419. Edward Elgar Publishing.

Grimmett, R.E. 2010. "Conventional arms transfers to developing nations, 2002–2009". *Congressional Research Service*, 10. Texts are available from http://www.fas.org/sgp/crs/weapons/R41403.pdf. Accessed 15 Feb 2016.

Hobe, S., Schmidt-Tedd, B., Schrogl K.-U., Goh, G. r. M. 2009. *Cologne commentary on space law*, 27. Heymanns.

Joyner, D.H. 2009. *International Law and the Proliferation of Weapons of Mass Destruction*, Oxford University Press, 40–43.

Kan, S.A. 2015. "China and proliferation of weapons of mass destruction and missiles: Policy issues. *Congressional Research Services*, 1. Texts are available at: https://fas.org/sgp/crs/nuke/RL31555.pdf. Accessed 19 Mar 2017.

Nikitin, M.B., Kerr, P.K., Hildreth, S.A. 2012. "Proliferation control regimes: Background and status". *Congressional Research Service*, 33. Texts are available from: https://www.fas.org/sgp/crs/nuke/RL31559.pdf. Accessed: 26 Feb 2016.

Sugihara, T. 2008. *Lectures on International Law*. 354. Yuhikaku.

Takaya-Umehara, Y. November–December 2010. "TCBMs over the military use of outer space". *Acta Astronautica*, 1299–1305, vol. 67, Issues 9–10, Elsevier.

Tronchetti, F. 2015 "Legal aspects of the military uses of outer space". In *Handbook of Space Law*, ed. Frans von der Dunk with Fabio Tronchetti, 334–335. Elgar.

Erratum to: Theory and Practice of Export Control

Dai Tamada and Philippe Achilleas

Erratum to: D. Tamada and P. Achilleas (eds.), *Theory and Practice of Export Control*, Kobe University Social Science Research Series, https://doi.org/10.1007/978-981-10-5960-5

The original version of the book was inadvertently published with the affiliation "International Court of Justice, The Hague, The Netherlands, k.nakajima@icj-cij.org", which has been now updated as "Graduate Institute of International and Development Studies, Geneva, Switzerland, kei.nakajima@graduateinstitute.ch" for author "Kei Nakajima" in backmatter.

The updated online version of the book can be found at https://doi.org/10.1007/978-981-10-5960-5

D. Tamada and P. Achilleas (eds.), *Theory and Practice of Export Control*, Kobe University Social Science Research Series,
https://doi.org/10.1007/978-981-10-5960-5_14

Theory and Practice of Export Control
A Conference Report

Kei Nakajima
Graduate Institute of International and Development Studies, Geneva, Switzerland
kei.nakajima@graduateinstitute.ch

On 26 and 27 November 2015, an international symposium titled *Theory and Practice of Export Control: Balancing International Security and International Economic Relations* was held at Kobe University, Kobe, Japan. This was the inaugural event of the International Group of Experts on Export Regulations (INGEER), organized by Kobe University and Université Paris-Sud, and sponsored by the industrial sector. The two-day symposium welcomed many participants so as to exchange views and to deepen their understanding on export control, both from the theoretical as well as practical perspectives.

After the opening remarks by Professor Dai Tamada (Kobe University), the first session chaired by Professor Vincent Correia (Université de Poitiers) discussed the topic *International Regime of Export Control.* As an introduction, Professor Philippe Achilleas (Université Paris-Sud/Université de Caen) presented a brief overview of international export control mechanisms, and explained how they are established and implemented. Among others, Achilleas highlighted the difference between export control and economic sanctions. The latter is implemented simply to restrict exports, whereas the former sometimes encourages export provided that it is properly implemented. His introductory talk was followed by presentations by Mr. Takuma Inoue (Ministry of Foreign Affairs, Japan) on the current situation of international export control regimes and Mr. Romain Broner (Airbus Helicopters) on the nature, function, typology, and legal framework of embargoes and international sanctions with special reference to the cases of Myanmar and BNP Paribas. Finally, Professor Masahiko Asada (Kyoto University) discussed the relationship between export control regimes and the UN sanction mechanism as introduced by the Security Council Resolutions 1540 and 1718. He concluded by highlighting the 'supplementary function' of UN sanctions resolution to export control regimes and 'effective synergy' between the two mechanisms.

The afternoon session chaired by Tamada focused on *Implementing Export Control in Business Scene*. After a brief introduction by Mr. Yuki Tanaka (Ministry

D. Tamada and P. Achilleas (eds.), *Theory and Practice of Export Control*,
Kobe University Social Science Research Series,
DOI 10.1007/978-981-10-5960-5

of Economy, Trade and Industry, Japan) of the Japanese Security Export Control System, Mr. Hisashi Riko (Center for Information on Security Trade Control: CISTEC) discussed the linkage channel connecting government, industry, and academia, and emphasized the role of CISTEC as a non-governmental organization within the triangle. The two overarching presentations were followed by papers on specific and practical topics. Mr. Arnaud Idiart (Airbus Group) focused on the management of country risk with reference to his experience at the Airbus Group, whereas Ms. Kumiko Kitayama (Toshiba) elucidated the practices of Toshiba in general. Dr. Marc Borello approached the theme from a contractual point of view. He argued a dichotomy of contractual approaches in dealing with export controls. The protective approach considers export control as a force majeure that leads to a temporary suspension or a termination of the contract, whereas the modern constructive approach attempts to avoid such consequences by exploring the possibility of changing the scope of the contract. The presentation made by Ms. Rosa Rosanelli (Pratt & Whitney Belgium Engine Center) particularly attracted questions from the floor. She discussed the effects and side-effects of the implementation of export control in the aerospace and defense sectors. The final speaker, Mr. Sandro Zero (Areva) simulated the audience by introducing 'The Botticelli Project'. He argued that industries, rather than governments, are well aware of how their dual-use products are used, resold and modified in the market, and therefore, industries should take initiatives for addressing issues relating to export control.

The third session, which was held in the second day morning and was chaired by Asada, discussed *Export Control in Relevant Areas of International Law*. First, Tamada attempted to broaden the scope of the issues to be discussed under the rubric of export control, by analyzing its relevance to investment and trade law. He argued that provisions such as exceptions, non-conforming clauses, national security, and public order in the context of investment liberalization (not investment protection after the establishment) could be relevant to export control so that this project should focus on these areas as well. Mr. Tomoaki Ishigaki (Cabinet Legislation Bureau of Japan) discussed Japan's recent revision of its arms transfer policy that allows more opportunities for providing defense equipment and technology, and concluded that this is the fruit of Japan's past experience, its current willingness to build security policy, and the practical need to address the changing security environment. Professor Mika Hayashi (Kobe University) discussed the relationship between export control and the Arms Trade Treaty and addressed the question as to whether the Treaty is able to prevent serious violations of international humanitarian law. The last two speakers addressed Air and Space Law. Professor Setsuko Aoki (Keio University) addressed the relevance of export control regimes to aerospace activities with reference to the Missile Technology Control Regime (MTCR), the Wassenaar Arrangement, and the UN Security Council Resolutions on North Korea referring to ballistic missile technology. Dr. Yuri Takaya (Kobe University) set the framework of the analysis 'Free Access to Outer Space versus Export Control of Missiles'.

The two-day symposium was summed up by Achilleas. In his concluding remarks, among others, he highlighted the notion of export control that refers to existing international export control regimes such as the Nuclear Suppliers Group, which is distinguished from export regulation that broadly covers both trade and investment law as well. Further, he differentiated objectives of export control: whereas the official objectives of export control include security, addressing trade protectionism could be a non-official objective. As the title of the symposium indicates, the ultimate goal is to balance the two conflicting interests of international security and free trade.

Each session reserved time for questions and answers, which deepened the understanding between the speakers and the audiences on the topics discussed. Also, receptions and dinners that provided an additional opportunity to exchange views were held on both days.

Index

D. Tamada and P. Achilleas (eds.), *Theory and Practice of Export Control*,
Kobe University Social Science Research Series,
DOI 10.1007/978-981-10-5960-5

The manufacturer's authorised representative in the EU is Springer Nature Customer Service Centre GmbH, Europaplatz 3, 69115 Heidelberg, Germany. If you have any concerns regarding our products, please contact ProductSafety@springernature.com

Printed and bound by CPI Group (UK) Ltd, Croydon, CR0 4YY
06/10/2026
02228868-0009